Building Common Faith

David Scott is a parish priest in Winchester and is Warden of the School of Spirituality in the diocese of Winchester. His three volumes of poetry, *A Quiet Gathering, Playing for England* and *New and Selected Poems*, are published by Bloodaxe. He is the author of *Moments of Prayer* (SPCK).

Building Common Faith

A Daily Commentary
on the Cycle of Readings
in *Celebrating Common Prayer*

David Scott

Poetic writing consists in letting
the Word resound behind words.

Gerhart Hauptmann

Today if ye will hear his voice,
harden not your hearts.

Ps. 95.8

The chief and top of our knowledge consists
in the book of books, the storehouse and magazine
of life and comfort, the holy Scriptures. There
we suck and live.

George Herbert

All one's own deductions from Scripture
are less certain than the words of Scripture.

Cardinal Newman

First published in 1997 by The Canterbury Press Norwich
(a publishing imprint of Hymns Ancient & Modern Limited
a registered charity)
St Mary's Works, St Mary's Plain
Norwich, Norfolk, NR3 3BH

All quotations from the Bible are taken from the *Revised English Bible* unless otherwise stated.

All quotations from the Psalms are taken from the *Celebrating Common Prayer* psalter unless otherwise indicated.

The front cover illustration by Sister Regina OSB is used by permission of Cassell Publishers.

British Library Cataloguing in Publication Data

A catalogue record for this book is available from the British Library

ISBN 1-85311-185-6

Typeset by David Gregson Associates, Beccles, Suffolk
Printed in Great Britain by Biddles Ltd,
Guildford and King's Lynn

Contents

Introduction

The practice of spending some moments after reading, or hearing scripture read, in meditative quiet, is an ancient one, and through the grace of God is being rediscovered. The barrage of words which come at us from so many directions, not least from the Church, has forced people to take refuge in silence; not to condemn words as such, but to be selective about them, and to allow them to be heard at depth. Words need silence, as lungs need air, but silence is not a quality in life with which everyone is familiar, and some feel it helpful to have their thoughts directed to begin with, even in a very simple way. Silence, then, is not a cold and threatening vacuum, but a warm and creative space, in which the scripture can take root and grow.

Several different responses occur as we rest in this silence. First, there is just that, a resting; but there could also be a thought about a particular situation relevant to the hearer; or a short prayer, winged to God; or one word repeated, turned over and about in the mind, and then allowed to sink into the heart; or a mental memo to look up a detail; or a commitment, or a judgement.

These brief thoughts on the readings suggested by the Cycle of Readings set out in *Celebrating Common Prayer* (pp. 341–430) are an attempt to help us focus on the passage, and might even work as well in preparation beforehand, as in meditation afterwards.

Being ready for a reading is a very good way of being sure it is understood. Following a brief description of the passage, I have added occasionally a quotation or a prayer; these are simply examples from my own meditations on the passages, and my hope is that others would find their own.

Two gentle warnings: one is that it has never been the custom in the liturgy of the Church, publicly, to direct congregations into a particular interpretation of a text before it is read, and it would not be right to use these brief passages as headings for the readings in church. Secondly, I have never found it helpful to take a pencil into church. It makes busy minds busier. Home is a different matter, and during a retreat or a quiet day, or alone in one's room, the pencil can come into its own, for noting down reactions to scripture and for writing down our prayers.

The main, but limited, aim of this commentary is to help you attend lovingly and intelligently to the daily readings in the weekday services of the Church. The practice of meditating on scripture used to be called *lectio divina*, 'godly reading', by the Benedictine communities who practised it most ardently, allowing scripture to fill their prayer and their work, and their sense of living together under God. Writing and reading in Winchester, once the home of a very creative Benedictine community, and through the centuries a place where scripture has been read, heard, sung, illustrated, and commented on, I am grateful to have been given this opportunity to continue, in a very minor way, that tradition.

David Scott
Winchester, 1997

The Cycle of Readings

Advent

WEEKDAYS FOLLOWING THE FIRST SUNDAY OF ADVENT

Monday morning

Isaiah 1. 1–3, 10–20

Israel's work is set from the beginning in a wide context of national concerns. The first of these is the pursuit of justice, rather than endless sacrifices.

Lord, help me to cease doing the evil that is ingrained like dye into my soul, and to do good.

Matthew 22. 1–14

The banquet is an image of the Kingdom of Heaven, and those originally invited are not the ones who taste the feast. In Matthew there is a strong undercurrent of the place of the Jews in the Kingdom, compared with the Gentiles, who are invited later.

Lord, make me truthful, unassuming, and humble.

*

Monday evening

Isaiah 40. 1–11

Commonly called Deutero-Isaiah, the themes of chapters 40–66 are Israel's redemption and her mission to the world. More particularly chapters 40–55 are an encouraging of the Jewish exiles in Babylon. They are usually dated shortly before the release of the Jews by Cyrus in 537 BC.

Praise God for his double mercies in pardon for our sins.

1 Thessalonians 1

The power of the Holy Spirit is very much behind the confidence of the church in Thessalonica. The gospel is not just a matter of mere words, but of the power of the Holy Spirit.

Tuesday morning

Isaiah 1. 21–28

What has become corrupt in the city will be purged. Justice itself has gone rotten, but God, the righteous one, will make the city of Jerusalem a Home of Righteousness.

Matthew 22. 15–22

'Herod's party' is a specific touch not often heard in the Gospels; it has a scorpion feel to it. They are out to catch Jesus with the sting of controversy. To what extent should we be this-worldly or other-worldly?

*

Tuesday evening

Isaiah 40. 12–end

In the difficult apprehending of God's nature, the writer acknowledges two things: one is God's unknowability, the other is his boundless strength and energy. We draw on that energy for ourselves.

Help me, Lord,
to soar as on eagle's wings,
to run and not feel faint,
to march on and not grow weary.

1 Thessalonians 2. 1–12

The hidden text is the complaint Paul has received about weighty authority, which Paul denies strongly, reminding the church of the affection in which he holds them.

Wednesday morning

Isaiah 2. 1–11

What seems like a vision of hope (vv. 2–5) very rapidly, like a stormy day, turns into a vision of despair (vv. 6–11), and then back into a modified optimism, in that 'the Lord alone will be exalted on that day'.

Matthew 22. 23–33

Then the Sadducees, who do not believe in a resurrection, ask about all sorts of this-worldly relationships. Jesus says, 'In the resurrection you will be like angels, so there is no need to worry.'

*

Wednesday evening

Isaiah 41. 1–16

God speaks sentiments full of hope for the future, rich in imagery and emotional power, to Israel his servant.

1 Thessalonians 2. 13–16

This is early Paul (51 AD) and the bare bones of his enthusiasms shine through. He is full of love for his early converts.

Thursday morning

Isaiah 4. 2–end

'Those who are left', the remnant in Jerusalem, will be covered with the canopy of God.

'God, my hope and my strength, a very present help in trouble' (Ps. 46.1, Coverdale).

Matthew 22. 34–40

Another story in the series of difficult issues. It shows Jesus coping and honing down his teaching to the very bedrock principles: love God and love your neighbour.

*

Thursday evening

Isaiah 41. 17–end

'The Lord speaks', but we can imagine Deutero-Isaiah writing these poetic prophecies for the liturgical services of lament held by the exiles. 'I roused one from the north and, he has come' is the great military and political saviour, Cyrus.

Lord, plant acacia, myrtle, and wild olives in our land and in my soul.

'You have put gladness in my heart,
more than when grain and wine and oil
increase' (Ps. 4.7).

1 Thessalonians 2. 17–end

There is a very strong sense of the imminent coming of Jesus, offset by a faith in that coming as a joyful coronation, not as a simple reward but as a sharing in the joy of the new converts.

✠

Friday morning

Isaiah 5. 1–7

This image of the vine and the vineyard, with God as the planter and dresser of vines, runs very deeply in the biblical imagination, and is picked up in John's Gospel.

Jesus said, 'I am the true vine' (John 15.1)

O Lord, who leaves nothing undone that is needful, still we spoil your vines.

Matthew 22. 41–end

This time Jesus asks the question, to elicit the response that the Messiah is far more than just a ruler in the line of King David. The Messiah is of God.

*

Friday evening

Isaiah 42. 1–17

The New Testament is the echo chamber for much of this chapter. The destiny of the chosen one, the one in whom God delights, the light of the world, the fulfiller of social justice, is all seen in Jesus of Nazareth.

O Lord, do not quench this smoking flax.

1 Thessalonians 3. 1–5

The reason for Timothy's visit to Thessalonica is explained: to help the church stand firm in faith.

Saturday morning

Isaiah 6. 1–10

The seraphim, glowing with love, and we lowly and unworthy under their feet, sing, 'Holy, holy, holy, the whole earth is full of his glory.' In such a setting, Isaiah senses his need for purity.

Lord, I too am a person of unclean lips.

Matthew 23. 1–12

Jesus stands out against hypocrisy, show, and pomposity, the things to which institutional religion is so prone.

*

Saturday evening

Isaiah 42. 18–end

Hearing and seeing are the senses which the writer most uses as indicators of a commitment and a closeness to the Lord; but hearing can be dulled, and seeing, blinded.

1 Thessalonians 3. 6–end

Timothy brings back good news of faith, and the love flowing back and forth is the natural outcome of a pioneering church and one that has a strong sense of unity under persecution.

Dear Lord,
what thanks can I give you back,
for everything in which you have spared all,
and waited for me until now?

✠

WEEKDAYS FOLLOWING THE SECOND SUNDAY OF ADVENT

Monday morning

Isaiah 9. 8–17

Speaking impiety (v. 17) – 'every mouth speaketh folly' (AV) – is compared with the Lord sending forth his word against Jacob, strong, direct and truthful. It is so easy to speak folly.

I must seek guidance from the Lord of Hosts. Lord be the keeper of the key of my lips.

Matthew 23. 13–22

The distinction is drawn between the heart of the matter and the outward skin or rind. Jesus is longing for people to get to the central meaning of things, the truth that is in God, because the truth sets us free.

*

Monday evening

Isaiah 43. 1–13

There is a very closely bonded relationship between God and Israel. There is nothing that God will not do for them, but that ironically increases the jealousy. 'I am the Lord, and I alone am your deliverer.'

'When you pass through water I shall be with you;
when you pass through rivers they will not overwhelm you;
walk through fire, and you will not be scorched,
through flames, and they will not burn you' (v. 2).

1 Thessalonians 4. 1–8

The way we must live if we are to please God includes an appeal to holiness, and a bar to fornication. Paul had recently experienced the worship of the Cabiri at Thessalonica, an immodest religious group espoused by the Macedonian hierarchy.

Tuesday morning

Isaiah 9.18 – 10.4

The anger of God is always a difficult trait for the contemporary world to understand. It is tied up with God's response to injustice and the urgency of the final judgement.

'It is God who judges;
he puts down one and lifts up another'
(Ps. 75.7).

Matthew 23. 23–32

An attack on hypocrisy is at the heart of Jesus' condemnations. The Pharisees set a bad example; they seem unable to see that the heart is the generator of faith.

*

Tuesday evening

Isaiah 43. 14–end

More images of both a fruitful future and an unfaithful past: contradictions which are probably accounted for by the placing of the texts. Deutero-Isaiah has a very keen eye for the future.

'Stop dwelling on past events
and brooding over days gone by.
I am about to do something new' (vv. 18, 19).

Thank you, Lord, for wiping out my transgressions and not remembering my sins any more.

1 Thessalonians 4. 9–12

Behaviour which increases love among the family of Christians (*phil-adelphias*) is also to be extended to those in the world, 'so that you may command the respect of those outside your own number'.

Lord, guide me by the spiritual teaching of the heart, to love others.

✠

Wednesday morning

Isaiah 10. 12–21

Out of all the ups and downs of obedience and disobedience to God, there will remain a remnant, a small group of people devoted to righteousness, and the worship of the Lord.

Lord, thank you for letting me lean on you.

Matthew 23. 33–end

Jerusalem stands guilty of being the city which murders the prophets. So much blood on its stones, then and now. The voices of wisdom go unheard and unheeded.

*

Wednesday evening

Isaiah 44. 1–8

Deutero-Isaiah is very much the mouthpiece of a strong and confident Lord, who is the first and the last, and the only God.

O Lord, pour out your spirit upon us; help us to grow like a green tamarisk, and like a willow by a flowing stream.

1 Thessalonians 4. 13–end

To 'meet the Lord in the air' is a wonderful thought, air being the element of the spirit, and therefore the right place to have a meeting. The final abode, said J. B. Lightfoot, is not described. It was enough to put the Thessalonians' minds at rest.

Thursday morning

Isaiah 11. 10–end

The gathering of the dispersed remnant into the one place is a great sign of the day of the Lord, and the rallying standard bearer will be the righteous branch of Jesse's tree.

Matthew 24. 1–14

Jesus warns his disciples about the signs of the end, and how they are not to be swayed but to be strong in faith to the last, for 'whoever endures to the end will be saved'.

Though 'the road winds uphill all the way', help me, Lord, to persevere with joy.

*

Thursday evening

Isaiah 44. 9–23

A discursive painting of ordinary life, rare in the prophets – or in the Bible even – makes a strong point about the triviality of idols.

1 Thessalonians 5. 1–11

The images of light and dark, day and night, remind us of Romans 13, in their capacity to evoke readiness for the coming of Christ, the midnight expectation of the Messiah.

✠

Friday morning

Isaiah 13. 1–16

Isaiah turns his attention to the surrounding nations: first, Babylon. Destruction will fall upon them in the day of the Lord. A scene of desolation, which leaves the big question, in a contemporary mind, 'How can God perpetrate such cruelty?' Is it a fate justly deserved?

Matthew 24. 15–28

Signs of the end, and the events of the end, are told. It will be divisive, sudden, and preceded by much delusion. 'The abomination of desolation' is thought to be a statue of the Emperor set up in the Temple.

*

Friday evening

Isaiah 44. 24–end

The redeemer and creator Lord turns things upside down. Jerusalem will be restored, Cyrus will be the Lord's anointed to fulfil the restoration, and our sins will be swept away like a mist.

1 Thessalonians 5. 12–22

In the list of wise things to do the nostalgic echo of the old confirmation prayer comes across: 'Be of good cheer, render unto no man evil for evil, protect the weak …'

✠

Saturday morning

Isaiah 21. 1–12

The prophet's vision is of a man highly disturbed in his passion and in his excitement. The date is about 550 BC. The torment is unusual: 'I have seen something but it is causing me great pain.' In the end all is restored in the cry of deliverance, telling of the fall of an important world power.

Matthew 24. 29–35

The dramatic scenario of the coming of the Son of Man is set among the warnings and the need to understand the particular time.

*

Saturday evening

Isaiah 45. 1–13

This meditation on the power of God as creator reminds us of the innovative power of the prophets, putting the word of God into the first person singular. Such was their sympathy with the Lord.

1 Thessalonians 5. 23–end

'The God of peace' slips so easily off the tongue … but of peace – not war, noise or enmity, but of peace. The same peace which we offer in love to our fellow Christians.

✠

WEEKDAYS FOLLOWING THE THIRD SUNDAY OF ADVENT

Monday morning

Isaiah 22. *1–14*

The fall of Jerusalem (701 BC) is caught here with the eye of a camera lens, amid the fatal cry of 'Let us eat and drink, for tomorrow we die' (v. 13).

Matthew 24. *36–44*

This resonant advent cry calls, 'Keep awake, then, for you do not know on what day your Lord will come.'

*

Monday evening

Isaiah 45. *14–end*

This is a God who walks in the light, because he made the light. He does not cower or hide, but is firmly on the side of the restoration of Jerusalem standing as a beacon of light among the nations.

2 *Thessalonians* 1

This is a letter to encourage and to build up the suffering church, and its individual members, in the faith of Christ.

'Our God will come and will not keep silence; before him there is a consuming flame' (Ps. 50.3).

May the name of the Lord Jesus be glorified in us.

✠

Tuesday morning

Isaiah 24. 1–6, 18b–end

It is a hard and uncomfortable truth to accept, but true, that we have laid waste our own earth, and are punished for it.

'The earth is empty and void
and stripped bare' (v. 3).

Matthew 24. 45–end

'Readiness is all', particularly in the light of the suddenness and unpredictability of the coming of Christ at the end.

*

Tuesday evening

Isaiah 46

The chapter rests on the vivid distinction between fabricated gods which need to be carried, and the God who is able to carry his people even to old age.

'Now that I am old and my hair is grey,
do not forsake me, God' (Ps. 71.18, REB).

2 Thessalonians 2. 1–12

'God puts them under a compelling delusion, because they did not open their minds to the love of the truth' (v. 11). This is like the passage in Romans 1 where God hands people over to their desires. There is a point over which people go, in which free choice of error becomes divine judgement.

✠

Wednesday morning

Isaiah 25. 1–9

This is a near-perfect parable of praise with that complicated extra dimension in the middle of the ruined cities. They are being brought to their knees in both senses.

'We have waited for him and he will deliver us.
This is the Lord for whom we have waited;
let us rejoice and exult in his deliverance'
(v. 9).

Matthew 25. 1–13
This watching and readiness for the coming of the Messiah has here the midnight theme. In the dead of night the light shines on the faithful. The bride and the bridegroom come together.

*

Wednesday evening

Isaiah 48. 1–11

Names of Israel, names of God, and 'I' appear here. 'I' is Isaiah speaking for God, God speaking through Isaiah, claiming the ultimate supremacy.

2 Thessalonians 2. 13–end

To possess the splendour of Jesus Christ is the purpose of all the suffering and the faith.

Lord, give me the courage to accept the cost of possessing your splendour.

✠

Thursday morning

Isaiah 26. 1–13

Isaiah on behalf of the city speaks up for righteousness and for the poor, with a shining jewel of prayerfulness in v. 9, where 'we' becomes 'I'.

'With all my heart I long for you in the night, at dawn I seek for you' (v. 9).

Matthew 25. 14–30

In terms of faith, a little will make more. The mustard seed will grow into the largest of trees, but to have no faith is to be culpable, particularly when it has been given, and the gift is then neglected.

Lord, help me to find the faith needed for your Kingdom.

*

Thursday evening

Isaiah 48. 12–end

More hope for the hopeful and less for the faithless, the division is again severe. There are strong echoes forward to Revelation in 'I am the first, I am the last also.' 'No peace for the wicked' has gone deeply into the language.

2 *Thessalonians 3. 1–5*

Faith in God and confidence in one another are the basis of the Christian community and of relations between different communities.

✠

Friday morning

Isaiah 28. 1–17

Over-drinking reduces the keenness of our making of judgements; this is straightforward. The tone of verses 9–17 is more difficult to fathom.

Matthew 25. 31–end

Abstract, intellectual faith is not enough to be on the right side of the divide. This classic depiction of the nature of incarnate love puts the emphasis on caring and on acting on behalf of the poor, the prisoners and the sick.

Lord, I believe; help my unbelief (Mark 9.24).

*

Friday evening

Isaiah 50. 1–10

The Lord is not to be blamed, that is clear, but whose voice continues after this? Is it Isaiah's? A new sound is heard here, deeper, more understanding and compassionate:

'The Lord God has given me
the tongue of one who has been instructed
to console the weary' (v. 4).

2 *Thessalonians 3. 6–end*

Often in this letter there is a very practical motive underlying the theology. Here it is the matter of work which overcomes idleness.

✠

THE EIGHT DAYS BEFORE CHRISTMAS

17 December morning

Genesis 3. 8–15

Nature and human nature are thrown into disorder as a result of disobedience to God's command. The symbol of this is the violent animosity between the head of the snake and the heel of the human.

Revelation 1. 1–8

'… what must soon take place … for the time of fulfilment is near … I am Omega – the end, the one who is to come.

Come, Lord Jesus

*

17 December evening

Isaiah 45. 2–8

The essence and the inspiration of righteousness comes from the Lord, and the Lord is eager to communicate his essential power to his people.

'Drop down, ye heavens, from above,
and let the skies pour down righteousness:
let the earth open, that they may bring forth
 salvation,
and let them cause righteousness to spring up
 together' (v. 8, RV).

Hebrews 10. 23–end

With the day of the Lord drawing near we are encouraged to look back to the days of suffering when our faith was strong.

✠

18 December morning

Jeremiah 29. 10b–14

Returning to a loved place, coming back from exile, can be a traumatic experience; but this time it is God's will. Those who seek will find.

Revelation 21. 1–7

'Now God has his dwelling with mankind' (v. 3).

God is with us, Emmanuel. This is the incarnation, the enfleshing, or embodying, of God in Jesus.

*

18 December evening

Isaiah 51. 1–11

Visions of hope abound, and in return, there is deliverance, and freedom from enemies.

'Gladness and joy will come upon them, while suffering and weariness flee away' (v. 11).

Lord, lift my weariness.

2 Peter 3. 8–13

See how the future tense affects the present. We are drawn on by the future coming of the Lord and that makes us 'think of what sort of person we ought to be, what devout and dedicated lives we should live' (v. 11).

✠

19 December morning

Jeremiah 30. 18–22

The joy of this passage is all the more powerful for being rare in Jeremiah. The restoration of things that have broken down comes not only in politics, but also in marriage relationships.

Revelation 21. 9–14 (15–21)

This dream-like picture of the new Jerusalem is packed with deliberately-chosen images. John puts the seal on the Bible (the Book), and trawls from the whole text for his imagery.

*

19 December evening

Isaiah 52. 1–12

The drama of liberation unfolds. We see a cramped and dispirited people, beginning to find and move their wings for the great flight back.

Jude, all or *1–4, 17–end*

To 'own' Jesus Christ is to be responsible for him, to stand up for him, to see things through in his name; but some 'disown' Christ.

✠

20 December morning

Jeremiah 33. 11–16

Part of the future peace will include a restoration of commercial and agricultural life: 'flocks will once more pass under the shepherd's hand as he counts them'.

Revelation 21. 22–end

A vision of the Kingdom is a vision of light and purity, freedom to come and go, and no intermediate buildings between us and God: no temple. The importance, richness and resonance of the Book of St John the Divine come with his working on the Book, the Bible, as a whole.

*

20 December evening

Isaiah 54. 1–13

The image here is not immediately easy to follow through. It is based on the ability of God to bring children to the barren, and to bring hope out of bleak despair.

1 Corinthians 1. 3–9

The coming, expected day is Jesus' day. He will rule, he will reward, he will be just and merciful.

✠

21 December morning

Zephaniah 3. 14–18

For the statement 'the Lord is among you as king' to resonate, we have to imagine the beauty, peace and order that the king maintained. It meant the end of fear, and the beginning of joy.

Revelation 22. 1–5

Of all the beautiful images of the Kingdom, this, with its fruit and water and light, the healing leaves, and worship, must be one of the most evocative.

*

21 December evening

Isaiah 55

This is a profoundly optimistic spiritual manifesto, in which the natural world provides an image of the goodness and beauty of the promises of God.

James 5. 7–9

Even James, whose epistle is well known for its insistence on good works as well as faith, here turns his mind to the coming of the Lord, which is at the same time the coming of the Judge.

✠

22 December morning

1 Samuel 1. 1–20

Here is a foretaste of Elizabeth and Zechariah, in the same temple environment as Hannah and Elkanah. As John is born miraculously to parents of old age, so Samuel is born to the sad and barren Hannah.

Revelation 22. 6–15

Such expectancy can hardly be contained. There is the nervous mistake of bowing down to an angel, the severity of the division between good and bad, those out and those in, and the excited interventions by John himself: 'It was I, John.'

*

22 December evening

Isaiah 56. 1–8

A very strong sense of the holiness of the Sabbath dominates here, as well as the holiness of the Temple.

Jesus takes up Isaiah's words, 'my house will be called a house of prayer for all nations' (v. 7).

Philippians 1. 3–11

Bringing good work to completion among members of the church has now the extra urgency that the day of the Lord brings.

Help me to pray to you, heavenly Father, with 'the deep yearning of Christ Jesus himself' (v. 8).

✠

23 December morning

Daniel 9. 17–19

Daniel's prayers are some of the most eloquent and moving prayers in the Bible. Here is one of them, with its particular emphasis on the urgency of the request.

Revelation 22. 16–end

I can't help feeling that John has taken on a special responsibility for the Book as a whole, to which he has added his own very special conclusion.

Maranatha:
Come, Lord Jesus.

✳

23 December evening

Isaiah 58. 1–12

This is a reminder of Matthew's Gospel, which concludes its material on warnings of the end (25. 31–46), by the division of the sheep and goats, depending on our acts of love. Isaiah strongly claims that the true fast is a matter of justice and love.

Philippians 4. 4–8

As the coming of the Lord, so is the end of life, and the coming of death. The Lord is near, do not be anxious. Pray, and God's peace will guard you, in Christ Jesus.

24 December morning

Isaiah 32. 1–8

'A king' and 'his ministers' is one more example of Isaiah being political through and through. His concern is with the wider world and its organization for justice and righteousness, against which is ranged the opposite, villainy.

Year A *Romans 16. 25–end*

Paul's concluding prayer to the Romans reveals that Jesus is the long-kept secret now to be disclosed.

Year B *Hebrews 10. 1–10*

The law is the shadow of good things to come. The good thing is the sacrifice of Jesus for our sins on the cross, for which and to which he was born.

'... born that man no more may die,
born to raise the sons of earth,
born to give them second birth'
(Charles Wesley).

Year C *Romans 1. 1–7*

Scripture moves towards this birth. The prophets point to it. It is both human and divine, and to it Paul is committed in love and obedience.

'All things are now complete which were spoken by the angel of the Virgin Mary' (Antiphon to the Benedictus).

*

24 December evening

Isaiah 62. 1–5

Images of hope tumble out from a voice committed to communicate: the sunrise, the crown, the wedding. Hephzibah was Hezekiah's wife, and the name means 'because the Lord delights in you'. It could possibly have been a proverbial title of endearment.

Matthew 1. 18–end

This key text in Matthew's description of the birth of Jesus is from Isaiah 7.14. The Hebrew *kalma*, girl, becomes the Greek *parthenon*, and then the English 'virgin'. It is crucial for Matthew's idea that Jesus is born of the Holy Spirit, although Joseph takes a loving and important part in it.

Christmastide

CHRISTMAS DAY TO 30 DECEMBER

Christmas Day

25 December morning

Isaiah 62. 11–end

The future tenses of this paeon of praise are hardly futures at all, they are as good as present: 'See, your deliverance comes.'

Luke 2. 15–20

The shepherds speak out, but Mary ponders and treasures up all that she is experiencing in her heart.

*

25 December evening

Isaiah 65. 17–end

Jerusalem, the holy mountain, is the focus of all expectation. To have such love for a city, such hopes for it, so many memories, is to take us into the feelings of Isaiah; and it is not just the buildings, it is also justice and the pursuit of fairness among the people.

1 John 1. 1–9

For 'word' read 'meaning', and think of the final line of Herbert's poem 'Prayer': 'something understood'. The peak of our spiritual life is to know, as we are known by God, to understand that Christ is the meaning, the word (Greek *logos*).

'Love is my meaning' (Julian of Norwich).

✠

St Stephen

26 December morning

Jeremiah 26. 1–5

Like Stephen, Jeremiah stands up to speak unpalatable words. Jeremiah foretells disaster if people do not mend their ways, and follow the way of the Lord.

or 2 Chronicles 24. 20–22

Zechariah, son of Jehoiada the priest, recalls people to their primary task of worshipping and obeying God; but they do not want to hear. So they stone the prophet.

Lord have mercy upon us, and turn our hearts to keep your law.

Acts 6. 1–7

Stephen was a man full of faith and of the Holy Spirit, and was chosen as one of the seven to distribute the widows' charity. So the basis for growth in the Church was the need to fulfil one of the basic commandments: 'Love your neighbour as yourself.'

✳

26 December evening

Genesis 4. 1–10

In the description of the jealousy between brothers, it appears to come from the Lord's prior favouritism of Abel's offering. What we read as cause and effect, the original readership would have understood as God's will being the only criterion for behaviour. God is supreme, therefore he has the right to choose. Similarly, for those who love God, death need hold no fear.

May my soul be pleasing to the Lord.

Matthew 23. 34–end

Jesus warns his disciples about the dangers of the 'end', and in a very human way weeps over the present situation and destiny of Jerusalem.

When I see Jerusalem and its fate, I think of our present cities, and sometimes even replace it with the name of a city I know well.

St John the Evangelist

27 December morning

Exodus 33. 7–11a (18–end)

God calls Moses out into the Tent of Meeting. The cloud is a sign of glory, and here prayer takes a dramatic place in the life of a person and a community.

Lord, thank you for those special places of meeting you.

John 13. 21–35

The atmosphere of love and betrayal surfaces among the disciples. John and Judas, as often in the Gospel, represent light and dark.

*

27 December evening

Isaiah 6. 1–8

The thrice-holy God, an embryonic Holy Trinity, sheds his glory over all the earth. Such glory evokes a deep sense of penitence. Sin is cauterized by one of the seraphim.

1 John 5. 1–12

The cryptic nature of verses 6–12 seems to be a halfway house, stylistically, between the purity of the Gospel and the tortured strangeness of the Apocalypse. What is the importance of 'the witness'? The witness is the one who proves the truth: see the truth in the baptism, in the cross, and in the sending down of the Holy Spirit.

28 December morning

Baruch 4. 21–27

It is God who will draw you back from the brink, and see your enemies defeated. Jeremiah has an intense involvement in the process of restoration.

'Take heart, my children! Cry out to God, for he who afflicted you will not forget you' (v. 27).

or *Jeremiah 31. 15–17*

Even the sound of the name 'Rama' evokes the cry of the distraught mother, weeping for her children. It means 'height', and we see and hear mothers of every generation grieving, in their solitude: for Benjamin and Joseph, as Rachel did, and for the children of the holocaust, Aberfan, and Dunblane. Yet, Jeremiah calls the tune of hope:

'Your children shall come again to their own border' (v. 17, AV).

1 Peter 4. 12–end

In the apostolic period the question of suffering for the cause of Christian discipleship is much discussed. To share in the sufferings of Christ is also to share in his glory.

*

28 December evening

Isaiah 49. 14–25

Place is so important in our relationship with God that to be exiled or moved away from a place we love can be felt as a bereavement, and we long to return.

Lord, none who look to you will ever be disappointed. Give us courage in isolation, to know that you will bring us home.

Matthew 18. 1–14

'You pass by a little child, you pass by spitefully, with a wrathful heart. You may not have noticed the child, but he has seen you, and your face, ugly and profane, will perhaps remain in his defenceless heart' (Dostoyevsky, *The Brothers Karamazov*).

✠

29 December morning

Micah 2. 12–13

The image of the sheepfold includes the gathering in and also the leading out, from the place of safety. The shepherd, in this case, is the Lord, their King.

John 3. 16–21

The incredible lack of grey areas in the writings of John leads to a great brightness of light, and an equally severe area of darkness. The deeds of darkness, and the deeds done in the light, are tragically portrayed in the martyrdom of Thomas Becket.

*

29 December evening

Isaiah 7. 10–14

'The light passing through a body, the body yet remaining whole: the light cometh through the glass, yet the glass is not perished. No more, thou, the light of Heaven, passing through, breaketh the glass; no more did the God of Heaven, by his passage, violate any whit, the Virginity of His Mother, if we will allow God the maker of the light, to do as much as the light, He hath made' (Lancelot Andrewes, Nativity Sermon, 9).

John 3. 31–end

Lord Jesus, you came from above and are above all; sent by God you speak the words of God; God gave you the Spirit without limit, the Son of the Father's love, into whose hand the Father has given all things. (From R. H. Lightfoot's *Commentary on St John's Gospel.*)

I want nothing but to know that in my heart,
so that I may live it in my life,
and wear it on my soul at death.

30 December morning

Micah 4. 1–5

This is a hymn to peace in which 'nation will not take up sword against nation', and the melting down of weapons of war will transform them into tools for work. It is always, in every generation, a hope that people will lay down their arms and 'go up' to hear the word of the Lord.

Lead me from hate to love, from war to peace.
Let peace fill our hearts, our world, our universe.

(From 'Prayer For Peace', adapted from the *Hindu Upanishads* by Satish Kumar.)

John 6. (5–14) 32–40

In these eucharistic homilies, the bread becomes life-giving and satisfying to all who come; and it is Jesus himself who gives it; and it is himself he gives.

*

30 December evening

Isaiah 10.33 – 11.12

The trees of Lebanon will fall with a great crash, a shoot will grow from them, and from that shoot a standard will be carved and raised to show the scattered people where to return to. When they arrive it will be paradise regained.

John 6. 41–58

In this most mystical of Gospels, the means to eternal life is through the process of eating and drinking. This is a fiercely fleshly route to the extremes of abstraction. There and here, then and now, God and humanity, join at the table.

31 DECEMBER TO 5 JANUARY

The Naming and Circumcision of Jesus

31 December morning

Micah 5. 2–4

Often the small things are set to overthrow the great, and so from Bethlehem, small among Judah's clans, will come a king.

John 7. 37–43

A dispute over the birthplace of the Messiah lights on Bethlehem as the place. In John's Gospel, with no birth narratives, this sort of confusion makes literary sense: the reader is not sure either.

'Streams of living water shall flow from within him': compare Zechariah 13.1 and 14.8.

✳

31 December evening

Deuteronomy 30. 11–end

'The word is very near you' (v. 14, NIV). It just needs to be attended to, taken in faith, and made ready to be kept. Once heard and understood, the choice is between making it your own and receiving 'life', or rejecting it and entering 'death'.

or Genesis 17. 1–12a, 15–16

The names of Abraham and Sarai indicate the Lord's designs: 'father of many nations', and 'mother of kings'. The sign of the covenant with Abraham is circumcision after eight days.

Luke 21. 25–36

Jesus' words, 'Heaven and earth will pass away, but my words will never pass away', give a wonderful confidence in the permanence of truth.

or Colossians 2. 8–15

Christ's way of circumcision is the stripping away of the old nature, and so the Gentiles are allowed into the ambit of God's love and forgiveness.

'It is in Christ that the Godhead in all its fullness dwells embodied' (v. 9).

✠

1 January morning

Isaiah 9. 2–7

'Eternal Father' (*Abba*) is one of the names of the child destined to greatness. The child will be the Father, an integration which St John saw vividly in Jesus: 'I and the Father are one.'

Acts 3. 1–16

Peter and John heal in the name of Jesus Christ of Nazareth. The ancient understanding that the power of the name, and that of the person, are interlinked, was felt and used in Acts, and still is in the Jesus Prayer of Orthodox spirituality.

Jesus Christ, Son of God, have mercy on me.

*

1 January evening

Jeremiah 23. 1–6

Two names or descriptions lie in this passage: 'Good Shepherd' (1–4) and 'The Lord our Righteousness' (5, 6). The Shepherd will care for his sheep, his people. The Righteous One will secure justice and security for the people.

Acts 4. 8–12

There is no other name by which we can be saved. A claim as all-embracing as that can only be lived to be proved. It is one thing to call on the name, another to live in it, and all it stands for.

✠

2 January morning

Isaiah 42. 1–9

Writing in the name of the Lord, with the Lord's agenda, assumes a remarkable affinity between Lord and servant. There are two servants here: the one who writes, and the other who is written about – 'Here is my servant'. How the Gospel writers lit on this text, to see Jesus as God's delight!

Ephesians 1. 1–14

These are benefits, listed in breathless delight, behind which lie a whole range of real experiences. Experiences of being blessed, released, given wisdom and the desire to praise, and all things 'brought into a unity in Christ'.

Lord, help us to see this vision.

*

2 January evening

Isaiah 43. 1–13

The word of the Lord offers hope (1–7), and Isaiah addresses the people (7–9). The Lord declares that 'You are my witnesses'. More and more I wonder what gives the impetus for a writer to speak so confidently in the name of the Lord – which, if you think about it, is the whole thrust of scripture.

Matthew 11. 2–6

Jesus does not claim Messiahship directly here. He points to the deeds themselves. John is expected to make up his own mind on the basis of the facts.

'Ye shall know them by their fruits' (Matthew 7.16, AV).

✠

3 January morning

Isaiah 42. 10–17

Isaiah calls people to rejoice, especially those with the sound of the sea in their ears, seafaring people of the coasts and the islands. The Lord is in his battle array (v. 13). Isaiah uses the image of birth for this quite new thing.

'Sing a new song to the Lord' (v. 10).

Ephesians 1. 15–end

The power and glory of God in Christ Jesus is effective for those who have faith. This couldn't be a more optimistic and triumphant image of God, far outweighing anything that ordinary human society could create.

*

3 January evening

Isaiah 44. 1–8

The name and nature of God in Isaiah traverses many themes: he is the one who fashioned us from birth; he is Lord, Israel's King, Lord of Hosts, Redeemer, first and last; there is no one like him; he is able to announce beforehand things to come.

Mark 3. 31–end

'Family' is redefined in terms of obedience to the will of God. Those 'sitting in the circle' around Jesus form an interesting and illuminating vignette into Jesus' 'style'. It is those 'in the round' who make up his family.

✠

4 January morning

Isaiah 42. 18–end

This is one of those passages where it is difficult to catch the tone of God's feelings towards his people, whether it is critical or praising. Or is Isaiah simply in turmoil as he writes, allowing his mind to thrash about?

'It wrapped him in flames, yet he did not learn, burnt him, yet he did not lay it to heart' (v. 25).

Ephesians 2. 1–10

'You once … but now': the high prospects and hopes we have in Christ Jesus. We are God's work of art, and have to grow into that great calling, not just aesthetically, but doing the 'good works prepared for us to walk in.'

(From the Prayer After Communion, Rite B, *Alternative Service Book.*)

*

4 January evening

Isaiah 49. 14–end

The Lord remembers Zion, and after all the failures and outrages, a new society will be born. Verse 25 is one of those verses which do not lie easily with contemporary views of God, but recompense and revenge seem to have been part of Israel's understanding of God's nature.

Luke 10. 21–24

A rare moment of uninhibited exultation by Jesus is captured here by Luke. It is in the Holy Spirit, and is a thanksgiving for revealing truth to the simple, and also to the disciples. It is a moment also of 'at-one-ment' between Father and Son.

5 January morning

Isaiah 33. 17–end

All sorts of good things are to happen, to the highest and the lowest. The lame and the blind will have an important place in the priority of care. So often in Isaiah, the vulnerable are remembered.

Ephesians 2. 11–end

With such a keen sense of the newness of being in Christ, and how different that is from the old way, this passage makes good reading for the new year, and for the new life, and for hopes for unity.

'Once you were far off, but now in union with Christ Jesus you have been brought near' (v. 13).

*

5 January evening

Jeremiah 31. 7–14

Many of the familiar images of bounty and celebration queue up to take their places: praise; being led to streams of water; the levelling of rough ground; the shepherding of the flock; the well-watered garden.

'Rejoice with those who rejoice' (Rom. 12.15).

or Baruch 4.36 – 5 end

'Jerusalem, look eastwards and see the joy that is coming to you from God' (4.36).

John 4. 9–26

The Messiahship claimed here by Jesus is one which provides the living water and is eternally refreshing.

Lord, give me this water, to quench the dryness of our lack of love for you.

or 2 Corinthians 4. 1–6

'... the light which is the knowledge of the glory of God in the face of Jesus Christ' (v. 6).

Deus illuminatio mea: Lord God, enlighten me.

If the Epiphany is observed on the Sunday between 2 and 8 January the following is used only as required.

5 January evening

Isaiah 46. 3–end

'I am God, and there is no other;
I am God, and there is no one like me.
From the beginning I reveal the end,
from ancient times what is yet to be' (vv. 9, 10).

2 Corinthians 8. 7–9

'Christ was rich, yet for your sake he became poor' (v. 9). Paul makes the claim for generosity between fellow Christians.

✠

6 January morning

Ecclesiasticus 24. 1–12

Wisdom and the law are joined here with memories of the Exodus, including God's presence in the cloud.

'It was I who covered the earth like a mist' (v. 3).

John 1. 1–14 (15–18)

'The Word became flesh' (v. 14): ordinary things can now become extraordinary. God becomes human, so that we can participate in God.

✳

6 January evening

Isaiah 48. 1–13

'From now on I show you new things' (v. 6).

'Sing to the Lord a new song;
Sing to the Lord, all the whole earth' (Ps. 96.1).

1 John 4. 7–16 (17–end)

God is love, and we must love each other with God's love. This love is the special, purified love which allows no selfishness. In Greek, it is *agape.*

✠

7 January morning

Jeremiah 31. 7–14

God, and the exquisite language of homecoming, penetrate the whole of scripture.

'But while he was still a long way off his father saw him, and his heart went out to him' (Luke 15.20).

Romans 15. 8–21

'Therefore will I extol you among the nations,
O Lord;
and sing praises to your name' (Ps 18.49).

Paul, the apostle to the Gentiles, gathers them in.

And may God, who is the ground of hope,
fill you with all joy and peace
as you lead the life of faith until,
by the power of the Holy Spirit,
you overflow with hope.

*

Epiphanytide

6 JANUARY TO 12 JANUARY

6 January morning

Isaiah 49. 1–6

The shifting identity in Isaiah is one of its great problems for the reader, and yet its most innovative aspect. The identity is both corporate and individual: one nation as a light to others, and the whole nation of Israel as the means of God's salvation.

Light is the great missionary power; the quality of light converts.

John 1. 29–34

John the Baptist's witness in this Gospel is very sure and strong. Jesus is the Lamb of God to take away the sin of the world. The chief witness to this is the Holy Spirit, and Jesus is revealed through the baptism as God's chosen one.

*

6 January evening

Isaiah 49. 7–13

Some of the imagery of the Psalms (23 and 121) is tucked away in this passage, suggesting a common store of images for describing Israel's hopeful future.

Lord, in all the glory of return, help us not to forget the practical issues of land, jobs, prisoners, and housing.

John 2. 1–11

The signs of St John's Gospel are signposts to the glory and centrality of Jesus, and a means of nourishing faith in the disciples.

Lord, you are the best wine, lately served at the feast.

Monday morning (or 7)

Isaiah 60. 8–end

'Who are these that sail along like clouds, that fly like doves to their dovecots?' is a beautiful and dramatic opening to the royal progress which is on its way to grace the new Jerusalem.

Ephesians 4. 1–16

Another procession, this time of captivity itself, which frees the Christian Church to be built up as the body of Christ.

In the body of the Church, help me to know what is my part, and how I may fit more humbly into it.

*

Monday evening

Isaiah 64

This lament coming in the middle of great hopes suggests an anthology of material, rather than a continuous story or outline of events. But the swing from exaltation to lament is so rapid that the editorial purpose becomes teasing. Personal responsibility for the situation comes out in v. 6:

'We all became like something unclean
and all our righteous deeds were like a filthy
rag' (v. 6).

Acts 11. 1–18

The progress of change to accommodate the Gentiles into the Christian 'way' here strikes at the very heart of apostolic authority. Peter is given a vision encouraging him to eat hitherto forbidden food.

Tuesday morning (or 8)

Isaiah 61. 1–9

The message of verses 1–3 cannot be extracted from its strategic position in St Luke's Gospel, as Jesus takes it on for his own missionary agenda. Jesus becomes the Lord's anointed. The title 'priests of the Lord' suggests a priestly or levitical background.

Ephesians 4. 17–end

'Learning Christ' is learning his story, learning his commands, learning his 'style' or mind; learning to internalize that in prayer ('putting on the new nature'); and then externalizing that in compassion.

*

Tuesday evening

Isaiah 65. 8–16

The remnant will be saved, but the majority will come under the judgement of God for dealing with chance and fate (v. 11), rather than the will of God.

Acts 13. 13–26, 44–49

The history of salvation, from the Exodus to the first people who acknowledged Jesus as Lord, concludes in this passage with the joy of the Gentiles on hearing that the light was shining on them. It remains selective; 'those who were marked out for eternal life became believers'.

✠

Wednesday morning (or 9)

Isaiah 61.10 – 62.5

The Lord's anointed, who in these passages merges with the voice of the writer, speaks, or proclaims. He cannot keep silent about the glorious things to come. It will be like the spring blossom and the wedding of bride and bridegroom.

Ephesians 5. 1–14

As well as an intricate theological mind, the writer to the Ephesians has a deep moral concern. The two come together here in the mystical understanding of the place of light in goodness.

Awake, rise from the dead, and Christ will shine upon you.

*

Wednesday evening

Isaiah 65. 17–end

There is a surprise in seeing the basis for St John in his Apocalypse here, but this borrowing is not unusual. Isaiah goes on with his social commitment for the poor and dispossessed, who will at last have the dignity of their own place in a new heaven and a new earth.

Acts 15. 6–21

The meeting between Peter and James leads to an agreement of sorts on the place of the Gentiles in the scheme of the Church. They are to be welcomed as the prophets indicated, but James lays down conditions to meet Jewish scruples.

Lord, let us cast the net wide to encourage disciples, as your disciples did for Gentiles.

Thursday morning (or 10)

Isaiah 62. 6–end

Jerusalem as a city is soon to be restored. The idea of a city as a whole being restored, both religiously and socially, is an example for us, so that the moral and spiritual quality of such cities may invite people to say they are 'Sought After' and a 'City No Longer Forsaken'.

Ephesians 5. 15–end

Let the Holy Spirit fill you.

Come Holy Ghost, our souls inspire,
And kindle with celestial fire.

✳

Thursday evening

Isaiah 66. 1–2, 5–14

The idea of Isaiah being married with three children gives a very human angle to the writing here. The Lord is seen as giving birth, suckling and rearing a people, with Jerusalem as their mother.

Acts 18. 1–10

Paul's great mission to the Gentiles held his whole attention and energy, fuelled by the lack of interest of the Jews in Corinth.

Lord, let me have no fear, but go on with my preaching, and not be silenced.

Friday morning (or 11)

Isaiah 63. 1–9

This great passage of the death, blood-shedding, and saving sacrifice of the Lord himself is also a great Easter passage. The question and answer prelude gives us a very powerful sense of involvement.

Ephesians 6. 1–9

Right relationships depend on mutual charity and respect. The art of leadership is to know how to follow. We all stand under the same Master.

✳

Friday evening

Isaiah 66. 18–22

The final verse of Isaiah (22) is a telling reminder of the otherness of his view of God's unsanitized, gloating, revengeful nature; but there are glories abounding in gathering the peoples to see the glory of God.

Acts 28. 16–end

Paul's final words underline his passion for the mission to the Gentiles, because of the hard-heartedness – as prophesied in Isaiah – of a section of the Jews.

Lord, help me simply 'to proclaim the Kingdom of God, and to teach the facts about the Lord Jesus Christ'.

Saturday morning (or 12)

Isaiah 63. 10–end

Isaiah takes the history of the Israelites and rehearses it in his own poetic way, and then longs for God to be involved still. The boldness of imagination is incomparable.

Ephesians 6. 10–end

God's armour is truth, integrity, peace, faith, and salvation, against unseen intractable powers of evil – chronicled in our own century by Kafka, Orwell, and Dostoyevsky.

*

Saturday evening

1 Samuel 16. 1–13a

Samuel anoints David as king, while Saul is still alive. David is away looking after sheep, but is summoned. This is an early example of the unexpected in the divine initiative.

Revelation 21.22 – 22.5

'The leaves of the trees are for the healing of the nations.' The nations are sick because of the rape of the trees. It is to the natural world that we often turn for sanity and wholeness, and water and light speak to us of God.

✠

WEEKDAYS FOLLOWING THE FIRST SUNDAY OF EPIPHANY

Monday morning

Genesis 1. 1–19

God creates a necessary division between heaven and earth, but this is not a spiritual division, merely spatial. Earth on the first day, heaven on the second – and heaven seems to be a convenient buffer between the waters above and below. The 'say' of God dominates this view of creation.

1 Corinthians 1. 1–9

Thanks, thanks and more thanks for God's Church (*ecclesia*) which is so full of talent and promise. The Church exists to make people ready for the coming of the Lord Jesus. It is a training ground, a school for 'the end'.

*

Monday evening

Jeremiah 1. 4–10

Beginnings always seem to go back further than we imagine. A birth is only a sort of beginning. The inadequacy of humans and the adequacy of God lead to Jeremiah's call to great things.

Luke 4. 1–13

The temptations of Jesus, each resonant of the barren heights where his forty days were spent, are rebutted by the tradition of holy writings.

These things you did, O Lord, for my sake, and I pray that you will now let me share in them, and they may be part of me: your fasting, and your temptation. (From Lancelot Andrewes.)

✠

Tuesday morning

Genesis 1.20 – 2.4a

The fifth, sixth, and seventh days follow, during which the human, the Adam, the prototype of Christ was created in the image and likeness of God, and also the blessed rest was sanctified.

'I am all at once what Christ is since he was what I am.'

(G. M. Hopkins, 'That Nature is a Hericlitean Fire')

1 Corinthians 1. 10–17

Beware all writers, preachers, poets who would 'rob the cross of its effect', by the vanity that lies behind most communication.

Lord, grant me the vigilance to let the cross speak its word of truth.

✳

Tuesday evening

Jeremiah 1. 11–end

The double meaning of the Hebrew word, translated 'almond tree' and 'ready to act', makes sense of verses 11 and 12. God's advice to a prophet could stand for anyone attempting honestly to do God's will.

'Though they attack you, they will not prevail, for I shall be with you to keep you safe' (v. 19).

Luke 4. 14–30

We can fix our eye on someone in curiosity, admiration, or hatred, and all three seem to be present here in Nazareth. Because we know the outcome for Jesus of being the 'one' who took on the prophetic role of Isaiah, we look with different eyes.

Give me, Lord, the closed eyes of penitence, the eager eyes of faith, the loving eyes of hope, and eyes lit by yours.

✠

Wednesday morning

Genesis 2. 4b–9, 15–end

More psychological and tactile than Genesis 1, the description here wraps a story round a problem. The problem is why people made by God are ill at ease in the world that was meant for them. Pre-science makes for vivid, simple descriptions.

Thank you God for making me earth, and breath, and for the glory and necessity of making both woman and man.

1 Corinthians 1. 18–25

The cross: is it folly, offence, or power? The message of the cross to us is that Christ is the power. It is not the wood, or the message, but the person of Christ that is crucial.

*

Wednesday evening

Jeremiah 2. 1–13

The great feature that the priests were judged on was that they did not ask the question, 'Where is the Lord?' Those who seek, find, and therefore to have in mind always, 'where is the Lord in this place, in this situation, in this world?' is one proof of a priest's faithfulness.

Lord, where are you? Show me where you are. Give me patience to wait for your reply.

Luke 4. 31–37

Jesus the teacher is thrown into a situation needing emergency help and healing. Teaching seems to be the undergirding task, and extra power goes out from Jesus on these extraordinary demands.

'Brief and concise come the words from him for he was no sophist: but the word was the power of God.'

(Justin, *Apology*, 1.14.11)

✠

Thursday morning

Genesis 3. 1–7

This has been such a fundamental text for our understanding of human nature and the purposes of God, for the way we see ourselves. The external temptation, with the internal assent to that, is the model.

Lead us not into temptation, but deliver us from evil.

1 Corinthians 1. 26–end

Being 'in Christ Jesus' is Paul's central vision. For our scientific view where two things cannot share the same space, this 'being in' seems impossible; but the foolishness of spiritual truth allows it, depends on it, relishes it.

*

Thursday evening

Jeremiah 2. 14–25

There are innumerable ways in which we are tempted to put God last rather than first. The 'foreign gods', what are they, for me, for the Church, for the world?

'You must have no other god besides me' (Exod. 20.3).

Luke 4. 38–41

Some illnesses Jesus locates and deals with as if they were human themselves, rebuking them. With other diseases he touches the person. Others are mixed up with the recognition of Jesus' Messiahship, and in Mark's Gospel Jesus wishes to silence them.

✠

Friday morning

Genesis 3. 8–end

The result of the act of human disobedience is a dislocation of relationships between humans and the created world of nature, and in the innocent rapport of man and woman. The over-stepping of limits set by God has been the source of temptation ever since.

1 Corinthians 2. 1–9

Human strength is made perfect in weakness. The real power of the world comes from what seems like powerlessness, and that is the cross.

O Lord, I have not yet 'learned' you, and do not yet know what it is to find you.

(After Thomas Merton.)

*

Friday evening

Jeremiah 2. 26–end

'There is blood on the corners of your robe – the life-blood of the innocent poor' (v. 34). Jeremiah's message is uncomfortable – now, as well as then.

'I will put my words in your mouth' (Jer. 1.9).

Luke 4. 42–end

'Proclaiming the gospel' is a unique form of communication, never simply preaching, or teaching, or healing, but containing all of these. It is the good news of the Kingdom of God; and what is that? It is that God is love and light and truth, and that is shown most clearly in the life, death and resurrection of Jesus, God's son.

✠

Saturday morning

Genesis 4. 1–16, 25

Something must lie behind God's blatant favouritism, some context rooted in the social or agricultural situation – together with an acute observation of the way brothers often behave. There is a development though from 'Am I my brother's keeper?' to 'if you say you love God and hate your brother you are a liar'.

1 Corinthians 2. 10–end

To possess the mind of Christ is to think our way through situations in Christ's way. It makes the background reading on the culture and times of Christ fascinating. To know as he knew, to look as he looked, is not just an intellectual task.

*

Saturday evening

Jeremiah 3. 6–18

This is a vision of a united nation, with Jerusalem at its centre. Israel is the prostitute who will have to be redeemed.

Luke 5. 1–11

'Signalling to our partners in the other boat' is what we should be doing more and more, to increase our mission and our strength of purpose; and then together we look to Christ, and follow him.

✠

WEEKDAYS FOLLOWING THE SECOND SUNDAY OF EPIPHANY

Monday morning

Genesis 6. 5–end

In all the wickedness of the world, Noah was the one blameless man of his time. The judgement of God here finds an elaborate and memorable story, which is universal and simple in its telling.

Let me praise you in the imagination of my heart.

1 Corinthians 3. 1–9

We are God's garden, and God's building. We play our part, but the real power for growth comes from God.

'Awake, O north wind; and come, thou south; blow upon my garden, that the spices thereof may flow out. Let my beloved come into his garden, and eat his pleasant fruits' (S. of S. 4. 16, AV).

*

Monday evening

Jeremiah 4. 1–4

I sense a deeper passion in Jeremiah even than in Isaiah: less poetry and more anger, and always uncomfortable.

'Swear "by the life of the Lord"
in truth, justice and uprightness' (v. 2).

Luke 5. 12–16

Christ is the one who can make us clean. His touch frees us from our diseases and our sin.

Lord, if only you will, you can make me clean.

Tuesday morning

Genesis 7. 1–16

God saved Noah and his family in the ark. The rains fell for forty days and nights, the same time as Jesus was in the wilderness, and the wild animals saved by Noah, surrounded Jesus too (Mk 1.13).

'The Lord is king above the flood'
(Ps 29.10, REB).

1 Corinthians 3. 10–15

'Except the Lord build the house
their labour is but lost that build it
(Ps. 127.1, BCP).

'Christ is made the sure foundation'
(J. M. Neale).

*

Tuesday evening

Jeremiah 4. 5–18

The wrongdoing of your heart, the harbouring of evil schemes, rebellion against the Lord God which is deep-seated within you – all this, says Jeremiah, is the reason why Jerusalem is about to be besieged.

Luke 5. 17–26

The healing of the paralytic man lowered through the roof turns into a conflict over the authority to forgive sins. Jesus has the power for both.

Lord, heal my sinful self, body and soul.

Wednesday morning

Genesis 7.17 – 8.5

The waters of the flood rise to clear the highest mountain by fifteen cubits. Everything is destroyed, and then the waters subside.

1 Corinthians 3. 16–end

From building to Temple: we are God's holy place, and our humanity is no cause for boasting.

*

Wednesday evening

Jeremiah 4. 19–end

The foolishness of not knowing God is one of the great causes of his wrath. The other is the self-concern for surface beauty rather than a deep obedience to God.

Luke 5. 27–32

The unexpected often surrounds Jesus' activities – the holy man attending a party with the unpopular and the undesirable.

'At length I heard a ragged noise and mirth of thieves and murderers: there I him espied.'

(George Herbert, 'Redemption')

✠

Thursday morning

Genesis 8. 6–end

Noah, his family and the animals are released on to dry and steady land, with huge relief no doubt. God's response to his flood is to promise that it will never happen again.

1 Corinthians 4. 1–5

We are stewards taking care of the things of God, until he comes. The urgency of our commitment depends on the immediacy and sureness of the coming of Christ.

Thursday evening

Jeremiah 5. 1–19

A hint of exile, at the very end of this passage, comes after a torrent of criticism about failing to understand God's purposes, committing adultery, not seeking the truth, nor acting justly.

Luke 5. 33–end

Both of these short sayings provide a fulcrum for true and false ways of seeing the evidence: feasting or not feasting, the old or the new garment. In each case we assume that Jesus is the bridegroom and the new garment, and the standards he speaks about are the standards of the Kingdom.

Friday morning

Genesis 9. 1–17

The rainbow is a beautiful symbol of a bond, or covenant, between God and humanity. It doesn't deny the problems of the rain, but the sun, the glory of God, shines through. So the fall is in some ways reversed by the covenant with Noah.

1 Corinthians 4. 6–13

Paul senses very acutely the humbling which is inevitably the Christian lot, but on reflection this is its glory. The cross turns all worldly standards upside down, like the tumbling clown.

Lord, if it be your will, let me be a fool for your sake.

*

Friday evening

Jeremiah 5. 20–end

These are body blows to the conscience, and clear statements of what we feared vaguely in our hearts: 'your wrongdoing has upset nature's order'; 'your sins have withholden good things from you' (AV).

Luke 6. 1–5

So frequently Jesus refutes his critics by an appeal to the precedent of scripture. In this case David eats the sacred bread. We get a picture of Jesus as one soaked in scripture.

Saturday morning

Genesis 11. 1–9

The logic seems so incomprehensible unless we keep in mind the very basic premise that God is in charge, his will must be obeyed, and anything that inverts that must be destroyed.

1 Corinthians 4. 14–end

'My example', 'you are my offspring', 'remember my way of life in Christ': Paul, who has been quite sharp against hero worship and division, here is very paternal towards the Corinthians.

✻

Saturday evening

Jeremiah 6. 9–21

Speaking and hearing are key senses in the world of prophecy. 'Behold, their ear is uncircumcised, and they cannot hearken' (v. 10, AV).

Lord, I have neglected your law.

Luke 6. 6–11

Sabbath stories abound. Jesus is keen to put the Sabbath in its rightful place. Other matters are more important, such as doing good.

✠

WEEKDAYS FOLLOWING THE THIRD SUNDAY OF EPIPHANY

Monday morning

Genesis 12. 1–9

Abram sets in motion, by command from God, the journey. The journey took hold of the Hebrew mind: Harran, Shechem, east of Bethel, the Negeb, longing to be settled, but never settled.

1 Corinthians 5. 1–8

Coping with the fierceness of Paul's reaction in this case is helped by knowing that it was the man's spirit he wished to save. The passage breathes a similar moral climate to our own.

Lord, that I may eat the unleavened bread of sincerity and truth.

*

Monday evening

Jeremiah 6. 22–end

Politics and prayer: 'See, an army is coming', and 'Daughter of my people, wrap yourself in sackcloth.' The only remedy to an oncoming disaster is personal and corporate repentance.

Luke 6. 12–19

The power of Christ, to attract his twelve, and to heal diseases, is the power of God: a power God makes available to those who love him.

✠

Tuesday morning

Genesis 13. 2–end

Another crucial division is made between Abram settling by the terebinths of Mamre at Hebron, and Lot settling among the wicked of Sodom. This is history seen through the eyes of its consequences, through faith and through sin.

What pleases God?

1 Corinthians 5. 9–end

Paul's great sensitivity is towards immoral behaviour, partly because he sees the destruction it wreaks in the relationship to God, and partly because he knows and sees the beauty of goodness.

Tuesday evening

Jeremiah 7. 1–15

Shiloh is set up as an example of apostasy, and as a warning to Jerusalem.

Lord, I know what I do matters; help me to do what matters to you.

Luke 6. 20–23

Dance for joy at the upturning of all expected values, says Jesus. The rewards will be great, and in the suffering involved there will be a solidarity with the prophets.

✠

Wednesday morning

Genesis 14. 1–16

In among all the kings and their armies, Lot is taken prisoner and then rescued by Abram, who in turn defeated King Kerdorleomer of Elam (present-day Iran). We don't often think of Abram as a soldier and captain of 318 retainers.

1 Corinthians 6. 1–11

You are to 'judge angels', and therefore why cannot you set up a system to judge one another in the Christian family? Wisdom is what is looked for, and purity of life.

Lord, I am not worthy.

*

Wednesday evening

Jeremiah 7. 16–28

'Obey me, and I shall be your God and you will be my people.' The result of moral obedience is a relationship with God. What begins as routine, ends with glory.

Luke 6. 24–26

Riches, food, entertainment, reputation: it sounds like the successful classes of any age. Beware – or alas, or woe, whatever the word – all of these things lead us away from our dependence on God.

✠

Thursday morning

Genesis 14. 17–end

God blesses the day of rest at the conclusion of the creation. God blessed Noah, and now Melchizedek, the priest, pronounces a blessing on Abram, on behalf of God.

1 Corinthians 6. 12–end

The body is a holy place for the indwelling of the Holy Spirit, and is for the possession, in marriage, of the other. Fornication trespasses on that union, and destroys its holiness.

*

Thursday evening

Jeremiah 7. 29–end

Harsh words rain down on the people of Jerusalem who have neglected the Lord, and (v. 3) indulged in child sacrifice.

Luke 6. 27–35

This is the wisdom of Jesus, and it is without compromise in its compassion. Putting love to the limit, is what the crucifixion did.

Friday morning

Genesis 15. 1–18

Land, animals for sacrifice, offspring: all these went to make up the Lord's covenant with Abram, but the most important element was Abram's trust. Paul's fundamental proof text for his message to the Romans comes here in v. 6: 'Abraham put his faith in God, and that faith was counted to him as righteousness.'

1 Corinthians 7. 1–11

Paul is responding to requests from the church at Corinth about matters of sexual morality.

*

Friday evening

Jeremiah 8. 4–17

'Yea, the stork in the heaven knoweth her appointed times; and the turtle and the crane, and the swallow observe the time of their coming' (v. 7, AV).

'Shall these swallows fly over me and put me in mind of my return; and shall I not heed them?'

(Lancelot Andrewes, Sermon for Ash Wednesday)

Luke 6. 36–38

The overwhelming generosity of God is always greater than we can imagine, and often greater than we will accept.

Saturday morning

Genesis 16

The story of the birth of Ishmael to Hagar and Abram is one more case of the outcome of events being read back into their origin. The outcome is conflict, so the intention must have been conflict. Raw reality is not avoided but, for us, it is strangely placed as the responsibility of God.

1 Corinthians 7. 12–24

Paul's Letters are a great mixture of theology and more practical matters. Here are examples of the latter: what to do about non-Christian partners in marriage, and the status of slaves.

✳

Saturday evening

Jeremiah 8.18 – 9.3

Jeremiah is utterly involved in the plight of his people. Their exile is felt by him back home.

'I am wounded by my people's wound.'

Luke 6. 39–45

The world of the carpenter's shop, the orchard behind the house, the building of the house opposite, have given Jesus the insights for teaching people about the Lord God.

WEEKDAYS FOLLOWING THE FOURTH SUNDAY OF EPIPHANY

Monday morning

Genesis 17. 1–22

Here are so many major decisions and demands: including the rite of circumcision, and the changing of the names, Abram to Abraham, Sarai to Sarah.

Lord, that I may live always in your presence and be blameless.

1 Corinthians 7. 25–35

'In a time of stress like the present', how should the Corinthian church members behave with regard to relationships? The ideal is in conflict with the realities.

O Lord, may I be beyond criticism and free from distraction in my devotion to you.

*

Monday evening

Jeremiah 9. 12–24

Paul echoes Jeremiah here when he says, 'God forbid that I should boast of anything but the cross of our Lord Jesus Christ.' God's boast, mediated through Jeremiah, is this:

'I show unfailing love,
I do justice and right on the earth' (v. 24).

Luke 6. 46–end

Rock and sand … The rock is firm: it holds, and stays, and helps others stay. Sand is shifting, transitory, easily dispersed. Sand is the word without fulfilment or commitment in deed.

Tuesday morning

Genesis 18. 1–15

The terebinth (Oak – Hebrew *elah*) 'of Mamre or its linear successors remained from the days of Abraham till the fourth century of the Christian era, and on its site Constantine erected a Christian church the ruins of which still remain'.

Tristram, *Natural History of the Bible* (1898)

See also Andrei Rublev's Icon of the Trinity.

1 Corinthians 7. 36–end

The state of virginity is a blessed one, and people enter it and remain in it by the grace of God. A restless virgin should marry.

'Because of the savour of thy good ointments thy name is as ointment poured forth, therefore do the virgins love thee' (S. of S. 1.3, AV).

*

Tuesday evening

Jeremiah 10. 1–16

The greatness of God and his creation are set antiphonally against complaints about the stupidity and disregarding nature of the Israelites. The passage has a liturgical feel to it, a ritual chanting of the good set over against the bad.

Luke 7. 1–10

Jesus responds to the faith of the centurion, based on the knowledge of his own job and responsibilities. Jew and Gentile mingle here in mutual respect.

Lord Jesus, signs of your saving love are all around us.

✠

Wednesday morning

Genesis 18. 16–end

In this dramatic dialogue, in which the Lord puts on a very human face, Abraham pleads for the innocent of Sodom, and God is merciful.

O Lord, you come and you go, you rage and are merciful, you come very close to us, and all for our sakes.

1 Corinthians 8. 1–6

Paul has a very enigmatic truth to tell here, tucked away in a discussion about meat: that is, that true knowledge cannot be known. If we think we have grasped God by knowledge, we are mistaken. Only love can enter the mystery of God.

O Lord, through you come all things, and we only really love in you.

✳

Wednesday evening

Jeremiah 10. 17–24

A personal cry of distress centres on flocks, tents, family, and the fear of the North.

'Correct me, Lord, but with justice, not in anger,
or you will bring me almost to nothing' (v. 24).

Luke 7. 11–17

Embedded in the story is the distinctive motive for Jesus' bringing back the young man to life: compassion for the bereaved widow.

Praise be to God.

✠

Thursday morning

Genesis 19. 1–3, 12–29

The absolute prepossession with God's judgement on sin reaches mythic proportions in the destruction of Sodom and Gomorrha. Lot's wife's nostalgia becomes a symbol of that judgement, carved in salt ... but Lot is saved through Abraham's prayer.

1 Corinthians 8. 7–end

Food is not just food; it can be a medium of compassion, or a weapon. We are asked to think of others' sensitivities as we eat.

Thursday evening

Jeremiah 11. 1–13

The heart is a crucial thing for Jeremiah. It can either be soft and obedient to God, or stubborn and wicked (v. 8).

Luke 7. 18–23

Jesus lets the eyes and the ears of the beholder and listener be the proof of his Messiahship. He does not force belief. He is the Way.

'... and generally a sound, sometimes a nod, is exhibited, the former to the ears, the latter to the eyes'.

(Augustine on the Last Supper, *Of the Trinity*, 15.10)

✠

Friday morning

Genesis 21. 1–7

The Lord who is the mighty one and of whom no image can be made, is the one who also shows favour, in a very human way. The incarnation is foreshadowed in this human aspect of God, and is underlined when God himself shows favour to Jesus at his baptism.

1 Corinthians 9. 1–7

Paul as married, Paul the man with the ordinary appetite for food and drink – that is on the one hand, and on the other an apostle, a free man, and someone who has seen the Lord.

✳

Friday evening

Jeremiah 11. 14–17

'Once the Lord called you an olive tree, leafy and fair …' (v. 16)

That is a beautiful aspiration: a hope from which we fall, as did Israel and Judah.

Luke 7. 24–30

Luke divides his history into separate periods, each with their own particular value: the time of the prophets; the anticipated time inaugurated by John the Baptist/Elijah; and the time of Jesus, to which all history looks, and which begins the royal reign, or kingdom.

Your Kingdom come.

✠

Saturday morning

Genesis 21. 8–21

The fate of Hagar and Ishmael is not easy reading, but, as with Abraham and Isaac, there is a terrifying and painful period before the favour of God is shown. This is similar to the 'dark night' of St John of the Cross and the anonymous medieval writer's 'cloud of unknowing'.

1 Corinthians 9. 8–14

Sorting out how to keep body and soul together in an apostolic life gives rise to some fairly stretched arguments. This is the part of the letter which could be labelled 'private business', and yet the gospel shines through a small crack.

'I put up with all that comes my way rather than offer any hindrance to the gospel of Christ' (v. 12)

Saturday evening

Jeremiah 11. 18–20

The autobiography takes its place here. It is reminiscent of the growing conflict between Jesus and the Jewish authorities in the Gospels. The pet lamb is led to the slaughter.

Luke 7. 31–35

This is the no-win situation that besets every generation, and here it centres on the attitudes to Jesus and John the Baptist, and their different views on asceticism.

Pre-Lent

WEEKDAYS FOLLOWING THE FIFTH SUNDAY BEFORE LENT

Monday morning

Genesis 22. 1–19

In this ultimate test of faith, Abraham proves himself worthy of God's promise. The test, as well as offering Isaac, was to trust that the Lord would provide.

'All nations on earth will wish to be blessed as your descendants are blessed' becomes the family tree of all faithful people.

1 Corinthians 9. 15–23

Not exactly 'all things to all men', but all things to the Jews, the Gentiles and the weak, to win them for the gospel, and thus to have a share in its blessings.

'It would be agony for me not to preach' (v. 16).

*

Monday evening

Jeremiah 12. 1–6

Jeremiah takes up the age-old cry of 'why do the wicked prosper?' He builds up a strategy for dealing with the problem that the treacherous present.

'Do not trust them, for all the fair words they use' (v. 6).

Luke 7. 36–end

This is another of Luke's two-character stories, where the actions of one contrast with the other. In this case, the love of the immoral woman, which issues from the experience of mercy, is set against the lack of hospitality from Simon.

Lord, give me the faith that will save me.

Tuesday morning

Genesis 23

Abraham buys a burial place from the Hittites, in order to bury Sarah. It is at Mamre, and becomes a holy place with sacred memories.

1 Corinthians 9. 24–end

An iron discipline underpins a fervent missionary activity, as ever.

*

Tuesday evening

Jeremiah 12. 7–end

Part of the huge anthology of liturgical 'woes' gives way here to a declaration that the reason for their being 'woes' is actually the Lord's doing. It is the result of a failure on our part to listen to God.

Luke 8. 1–3

We give you thanks, O Lord, for those who support us, in known and unknown ways.

✠

Wednesday morning

Genesis 24. 1–9

Abraham wants Isaac to marry a girl from his own family and country, not from Canaan. The servant plays a crucial role in this matchmaking. He bears the blessings of the Lord.

1 Corinthians 10. 1–13

Paul looks on events of the distant past as symbolic of the actions, particularly in the Last Supper, of Christ. He calls them 'supernatural', having meanings deeper than the outward action. It was a way of biblical interpretation deeply ingrained in the New Testament writers, and beyond.

*

Wednesday evening

Jeremiah 13. 1–14

This is a simple acted parable of the way that the Lord is going to ruin the enormous pride of Judah and Jerusalem: like a loincloth spoiled, like wine-jars smashed.

Luke 8. 4–15

At the core of the gospel is the need to communicate it. The sower of seed is the prime image for this process, around which many subsidiary pictures have gathered (e.g. 'those on rocky ground').

Lord, may your gospel be rooted in good ground.

✠

Thursday morning

Genesis 24. 10–27

The well was no doubt one of the great meeting places of the day, but the combination of drawing fresh water and the seeds of a marriage makes the whole scene rich in blessings and in images. Rebecca was very beautiful, and a virgin. A bell rings forward to Mary.

1 Corinthians 10. 14–22

The relationship of Jewish sacrifice to the worship of the Early Church is taken much further in the Letter to Hebrews. The Eucharist is distinguished from idolatry by the presence of Christ.

'Though we are many, we are one body' (from the ASB Communion Service).

*

Thursday evening

Jeremiah 13. 20–end

The north is the source of fear and attack, used by the Lord to humble Jerusalem. Nakedness is a strong image here of the suffering and shame they are going to have to endure. Jesus' nakedness on the cross is an undoing of this.

Luke 8. 16–18

The secretive nature of Mark's Gospel is here, in Luke's, overturned into a public gospel. Luke very much wants people to see, be touched in their heart, believe, and then follow their Lord and Master.

✠

Friday morning

Genesis 24. 28–51

All happens under the moving spirit of the Lord, and according to the will of his faithful servant Abraham. Laban and Bethuel let Rebecca go.

'Since this is from the Lord, we can say nothing for or against it' (Gen. 24.50).

'Be it unto me according to your word' (Luke 1.38).

1 Corinthians 10. 23–30

What builds up a community? The community here is the Corinthian Christians, held together by the gospel, and the sharing of Christ's body and blood, in the form of bread and wine.

Lord, is it for the good of your community?

*

Friday evening

Jeremiah 14. 1–10

'You are among us, O Lord,
and we are called by your name.
Leave us not, O Lord our God' (v. 9).
(Adapted from the service of Compline.)

Luke 8. 19–21

The word of God is the main source of commitment, transcending all others, and the task is to allow that to be the wellspring for action.

✠

Saturday morning

Genesis 24. 52–end

The providential element in the story is very strong: the journey, the sighting by Isaac of the camels, the veiling, the tent.

'You are our sister, may you be the mother of
many children;
may your sons possess the cities of their
enemies' (v. 60).

1 Corinthians 10.31 – 11.1

'... try to be considerate to everyone ...' (v. 33) Paul had his conflicts and his troubles with people, and with this principle in his heart he would sometimes have been torn apart.

*

Saturday evening

Jeremiah 14. 11–end

The uncompromising God puts pay to all sentimental covering up of the truth. Rather, say:

'Let my eyes stream with tears,
ceaselessly night and day' (v. 17)

but

'Is it not in you, Lord our God,
that we put our hope?' (v. 22)

Luke 8. 22–25

In the storms of living, where is our faith? Our faith is in you, O God: our shore, our peace.

'Never weather-beaten sail
More willing bent to shore'
(Thomas Campion).

✠

WEEKDAYS FOLLOWING THE FOURTH SUNDAY BEFORE LENT

Monday morning

Genesis 25. 7–11

As in many a country churchyard, Abraham joins his wife in death, buried in the cave at Machpelah. The blessing of God then rests on Isaac.

1 Corinthians 11. 2–16

This is one of those passages that, while it has dated irreparably in the western church, still retains its vestiges in the east, for better or worse, and is the voice of Paul under the stress of conflict in the church.

*

Monday evening

Jeremiah 15. 1–9

Now the Lord names names: Manasseh, son of Hezekiah, King of Judah. It is his crimes that have brought the Lord to do what he must do. It is a harsh and cruel passage, but will it bring us to 'turn'?

Luke 8. 26–39

Jesus claims the tempest of the waves and the tempest of the mind. The Prince of Peace casts out demons by the finger of God.

Lord, take my mind and think through it.

✠

Tuesday morning

Genesis 25. 19–28

Tracing the blessing of the Lord is the work of the writer here; and the events of the lives of Esau and Jacob are described with this in mind.

'The elder will be servant to the younger' (v. 23).

1 Corinthians 11. 17–end

Out of the squabbles and divisions of the church at Corinth comes this jewel of early eucharistic practice. Proclaiming the death of the Lord became the central focus of Reformation eucharistic thought, and the ethos of the Communion Service in the *Book of Common Prayer*.

'Almighty God, our heavenly Father, who of thy tender mercy didst give thine only Son Jesus Christ to suffer death upon the cross for our redemption ...' (BCP)

*

Tuesday evening

Jeremiah 15. 10–end

Three different sorts of voices are heard here: the voice of the Lord; Jeremiah speaking the word of the Lord; and Jeremiah himself. Three different spoken voices would help us distinguish more clearly. The Lord intimately reassuring Jeremiah is very moving.

'If you turn back to me, I shall take you back' (v. 19).

Luke 8. 40–42, 49–end

If Jesus is the breath of the Kingdom then we should expect him to be breathing new life into the world, a foretaste of the reality of life with God, in which we shall all be able to awake from sleep and stand.

✠

Wednesday morning

Genesis 25. 29–end

The story of the 'mess of pottage' or 'red broth' confirms the idea that Esau will be subservient to Jacob, through the selling of the birthright.

1 Corinthians 12. 1–3
No one with the Spirit of God can say 'A curse on Jesus!'; no one without the Holy Spirit can say 'Jesus is Lord!'

*

Wednesday evening

Jeremiah 16. 1–13

Anger comes out of difficult and troubled times. It is a very real emotion and God shows it to the full. We have to fill in the emotional and social background against which God's anger is set.

Luke 8. 43–48

Power goes out from Jesus in healing: tangible power for good, and power which is shy of noise and acclaim.

'Who was it who touched me?'
It was me, Lord.

Thursday morning

Genesis 27. 1–17

The birthright is one thing, the deathbed blessing another. Rebecca engineers the deceit, and it seems a far cry from the beauty of the first meeting with Isaac at the well.

1 Corinthians 12. 4–11

The Spirit indwells a person, making them more what they are meant to be, crowning their gift, and using it for the good of all.

Lord, thank you for my gift, even if it is only having the desire to love you.

Thursday evening

Jeremiah 16. 14–end

There is historical movement here back and forward. The scattered people will be brought back to Jerusalem in a new Exodus, and on returning will be punished for their sins, and given another chance.

'Lord, my strength and my stronghold,
my refuge in time of trouble' (v. 19).

Luke 9. 1–6

It really must have been good news for the apostles or they wouldn't have been prepared to give up their lives for the gospel. Proclaiming the nearness of God and healing the sick was their task.

Lord, help us in this task, today.

Friday morning

Genesis 27. 18–29

The charade continues: Rebecca's scheming, Jacob's connivance, Isaac's blindness and age, his speech about the blessings of the country; and then his great blessing, so misplaced:

'A curse on those who curse you,
but a blessing on those who bless you!' (v. 29)

1 Corinthians 12. 12–26

The different parts of the body working together is probably a universal image, used here by Paul to great effect, for describing the sharing of different gifts, and the sense of mutual joy and sorrow.

Friday evening

Jeremiah 17. 5–10

Jeremiah is the psalmist and the poet without fear; his eyes are always alert for any sign of idolatry, any putting 'trust in mortals' before God.

Luke 9. 7–9

Jesus was an absolutely integral part of the closeness of God in the coming of the Kingdom. Even Herod had heard of this, and is one of the protagonists who unwittingly becomes a witness.

✠

Saturday morning

Genesis 27. 30–40

Timing and the relentless movement of fortune are two great elements of tragedy. Esau was just too late, and even from the beginning was not favoured by the Lord.

'One will be taken, the other left' (Matt. 24.41).

1 Corinthians 12. 27–end

'You are Christ's body': but in the list neither priests nor lay people appear, but apostles and prophets. The apostles are sent out to proclaim the closeness of the Kingdom of God, and the prophets are those who listen to the word of God and declare it.

Saturday evening

Jeremiah 17. 19–end

Jeremiah is adamant about the importance of the Sinai commandments: worshipping God alone, and keeping the Sabbath holy. 'Holy' is being dedicated to the love and worship of God.

Luke 9. 10–17

Kingdom and healing stand side by side again. In the feeding of the five thousand what Jesus gives, satisfies, and his love is experienced as excess, filling the twelve baskets of the new Israel, which should be seen as the Church.

✠

WEEKDAYS FOLLOWING THE THIRD SUNDAY BEFORE LENT

Monday morning

Genesis 27. 41–45

Imagine it in contemporary dress. There is something universal about a mother's managing of two sons.

1 Corinthians 13

This *agape*, this special sort of love, is from God, but it is never out of the reach or range of ordinary, daily relationships.

*

Monday evening

Jeremiah 18. 1–12

God is like a potter, in charge of the destiny of the clay. The clay is the House of Israel. How good that a community should have its own potter!

'Turn back, every one of you, from his evil conduct; mend your ways and your actions' (v. 11).

Luke 9. 18–22

Jesus' prayer leads to a question of identity: 'Who do the people say I am?' Jesus knows that whatever anyone else says, he has a destiny to suffer, die, and rise again.

✠

Tuesday morning

Genesis 28. 1–5

So Jacob is sent by Isaac, with his blessing, to Paddan-Áram, to Laban, son of Bethuel, to find a wife. The cycle of birth, marriage and death continues, but in these stories God is always on the journey too.

1 Corinthians 14. 1–12

Paul puts comprehensibility very high on his list of gifts. The prophet speaks so that people can understand and be moved into right action by his words. This is the outward dimension, not just self-satisfying spiritual experience.

⁂

Tuesday evening

Jeremiah 18. 18–end

What it is like to be really threatened is well charted here, as in many of the psalms.

'I am forgotten like the dead, out of mind;
I am as useless as a broken pot' (Ps. 31.12).

Luke 9. 23–27

'Take up your cross and follow me.' Did we once imagine it would be an easy ride?

✠

Wednesday morning

Genesis 28. 10–end

The land, the place, and the presence of God are all intimately brought together in this numinous passage. The ladder became a familiar mystical theme for what tied God to earth, and earth to heaven.

1 Corinthians 14. 13–19

Mind and heart ... but mind, here, is a corrective, a balance, a redress, to what might have been an over-enthusiastic, indulgent worship style.

'You must love the Lord your God ... with all your mind (Mark 12.30).

✳

Wednesday evening

Jeremiah 19

Jeremiah makes impressive major statements, based on quite small domestic images. A pot breaking is symbolic of a wholesale destruction of a community, because they have been offering child sacrifices to Baal.

O Lord, give me the time to listen to you.

Luke 9. 28–36

There is no glory without suffering. It is in the context of Jesus' teaching on the cross that this visionary experience occurs. Equally there is no glorified Jesus without Moses and Elijah. Past and present take us together, into the future.

✠

Thursday morning

Genesis 29. 1–14

Jacob arrives at 'the land of the eastern tribes', and beside the source of fresh water Rachel appears, coming with the flock.

'And Jacob kissed Rachel, and lifted up his voice, and wept' (v. 11, AV).

1 Corinthians 14. 20–25

'Prophecy' is an important word here. It is obviously not just telling the future, but speaking intelligently and helpfully about the way God is involved in the world now. It must lead the stranger to say as he confronts it in worship:

'God is certainly among you!' (v. 25)

Thursday evening

Jeremiah 20. 1–6

To fight for what is right and to suffer on behalf of the Lord,
Let us pray to the Lord.

Luke 9. 37–43

Down from the mountain into the valley ... Jesus senses a lack of faith, and you feel he is really digging deep into his resources in a difficult time to cast out the unclean spirit.

✠

Friday morning

Genesis 29. 15–30

Duplicity is mingled in with the beauty of Jacob's love for Rachel. Nothing is unalloyed joy, and again there are two people, Leah and Rachel, one favoured by God more than the other.

1 Corinthians 14. 26–33

'God is not a God of disorder but of peace.' That is the test.

*

Friday evening

Jeremiah 20. 7–end

This lament goes up and down, and in and out of joy and sorrow, anger and submission. There is no denying Jeremiah's involvement with the living God and with a troubled world.

'But the Lord is on my side,
a powerful champion' (v. 11).

Luke 9. 44–45

The disciples felt they should know. Things were getting tense. Everything was happening at once, and the sense of foreboding – 'the Son of Man is to be given up into the power of men' – had no clear focus for them yet.

✠

Saturday morning

Genesis 30. 25–end

However the process worked of getting the right sheep to mate, Jacob comes out of the deal a richer man, no thanks to Laban. The wealth was in the flocks.

1 Corinthians 14. 34–end

'Let all be done decently and in order' (v. 40) – which brings us back to love, and concern for the feelings of others and for the communal sense of what is fitting.

✳

Saturday evening

Jeremiah 21. 1–10

Speak the truth even before kings, even if it involves a prophecy of disaster. Jerusalem and all the power structure will be handed over to Nebuchadrezzar of Babylon.

Luke 9. 46–50

If ever the phrase 'gentle Jesus' was fulfilled, it is here. It is certainly not the whole picture of the man, but who would have such a way with children unless there was a gentle spirit? Children sense.

✠

WEEKDAYS FOLLOWING THE SECOND SUNDAY BEFORE LENT

Monday morning

Genesis 31. 1–21

The God of Bethel oversees the fortunes of Jacob. The Lord who comes in a dream also comes to sort out the spotted sheep.

1 Corinthians 15. 1–11

Paul has no embarrassment about the gospel, only about his authority in coming late to the apostles. He passes on the tradition:

Christ died for our sins …
was buried …
was raised to life on the third day …
was seen by Peter and then by the twelve
(vv. 3–5).

✳

Monday evening

Jeremiah 22. 1–5, 13–19

'Think of your father …
He upheld the cause of the lowly and the poor;
then all was well' (vv. 15, 16).

Josiah was the father, Shallum the son.

Luke 9. 51–56

'Resolutely': no haphazard wandering, nor off-chance speculation, but Jesus had made up his mind. This was both the beginning of the end, and the beginning of a new beginning.

✠

Tuesday morning

Genesis 31. 22–42

Rebecca sits on the stolen household gods, hiding them from Laban and claiming to have 'the common lot of woman upon her'. How future generations must have enjoyed telling these stories.

1 Corinthians 15. 12–19

The resurrection is the cornerstone of the proclamation, and is received by faith. You cannot perceive the resurrection without faith.

'If Christ was not raised, then our gospel is null and void' (v. 14).

*

Tuesday evening

Jeremiah 22. 20–end

'Land, land, land! Hear the words of the Lord' (v. 29). The land is Judah under Coniah, son of Jehoiakim.

Luke 9. 57–end

A selection of quite tough sayings fits in with the resolution Jesus is now showing. Resolution demands commitment.

✠

Wednesday morning

Genesis 31.43 – 32.2

A dispute between Jacob and Laban is sorted out by a division of territory.

'Good walls make good neighbours' (Robert Frost).

1 Corinthians 15. 20–28

The glory and the joy of the resurrection breathe through these words. We feel better than we did before. Death has been defeated. 'God will be all in all.'

*

Wednesday evening

Jeremiah 23. 1–8

The shepherds are encouraged to care for the sheep. The Lord will rescue a remnant, and the Good Shepherd, a branch of David's line, will be King and rule wisely. How eagerly this passage was scored by the Early Church.

Luke 10. 1–16

The prophets were killed in Jerusalem and Jesus has the prophetic sound in his voice: 'Alas for you!'

✠

Thursday evening

Genesis 32. 3–22

Jacob is really nervous about meeting Esau. The prayer in vv. 9–11 is a classic one:

'God of my father Abraham …
I am not worthy of all the
true and steadfast love …
Save me, I pray, from my brother Esau.'

1 Corinthians 15. 29–34

Ideas are flying about here in the white heat of enthusiasm over the intense reality of the resurrection.

'Every day I die' (v. 31).

✳

Thursday evening

Jeremiah 23. 9–17

'Within my breast my heart gives way.' There is a relentless pursuit of the wicked and faithless, and no wonder Jeremiah so constantly loses heart. We do, for far less cause.

Luke 10. 17–24

Sonship of the Father in heaven is Jesus' most intimate relation, and how he understands himself. It is a secret he shares with his closest friends.

✠

Friday morning

Genesis 32. 22–end

Who is Jacob wrestling with? His own conscience, a man, an angel? Whoever it was, he refused Jacob his name, but not his blessing.

1 Corinthians 15. 35–50

What will get us behind the patina of countless funeral services, to see these thoughts freshly written? 'Sown a physical body, it is raised a spiritual body.' The one is as far from, and as close to, the other as a seed is to a flower.

*

Friday evening

Jeremiah 23. 18–29

No, Lord! You are a God both near and far away. We cannot hide in a secret place and not be seen by you. You fill heaven and earth.

Luke 10. 25–37

We perhaps do not get the shock of the goodness of the Samaritan, or his excessive generosity because we read the story through a changed attitude to Samaritans, which the parable itself helped to engender. The lawyer, gummed up with the law, needs to be involved with the surprise of love.

✠

Saturday morning

Genesis 33. 1–18

Jacob makes amends with Esau, through gifts. The tension slips away, and they go their separate ways: Jacob to Shechem, where he builds an altar. Building altars is the job of the holy.

1 Corinthians 15. 51–end

This is a victory speech, with Paul's particular interest in v. 56: 'sin gains its power from the law'. Change is the great excitement about which, here below, we are so fearful.

Saturday evening

Jeremiah 24

This great leap in the relationship between God and his faithful people could be called the covenant of the heart: 'And I will give them a heart to know that I am the Lord, and they shall be my people and I will be their God' (v. 7, RV).

Luke 10. 38–end

The busy, practical Samaritan is commended. The busy, practical Martha is cautioned. Sitting at the feet of Jesus, hearing his words, being full of dedication and passionate, contemplative listening is commended too. Mary of Bethany is its epitome.

WEEKDAYS FOLLOWING THE SUNDAY BEFORE LENT

Monday morning

Genesis 35. 1–15

Bethel (Luz), in Canaan, was a crucial and holy place in early Hebrew faith. It was the place of the altar set up by Jacob.

O God, you are the one who assisted me in my distress, and who has been with me wherever I have gone.

1 Corinthians 16. 1–12

Paul deals with various practical matters including 'the collection' for the Christians in Jerusalem.

*

Monday evening

Jeremiah 25. 1–14

Over a quarter of a century, Jeremiah has been advising his people, but they have not listened, and judgement will come in the form of conquest by a foreign power.

Luke 11. 1–13

A section on prayer, mainly describing what to ask for from God, also describes God as the loving Father who provides for his children.

Abba, Father.

✠

Tuesday morning

Genesis 35. 16–20

Jacob buries his wife Rachel 'by the side of the road'. They were on a journey from Bethel to Ephrathah. She died giving birth to Ben-oni, renamed by Jacob, Benjamin.

Lord, be with those who even today will be dying at the side of the road.

1 Corinthians 16. 13–end

The kiss of peace is so right and easy in some contexts, and so difficult in others. How easy and vital when we share a common sense of trial or danger, and how difficult when we are self-sufficient and independent.

Maranatha. Come, Lord.

*

Tuesday evening

Jeremiah 25. 15–16, 27–end

The cup of suffering which makes Jerusalem and Judah sick with drunkenness, is the cup of their own sin. The cup which Jesus drinks in the Garden of Gethsemane is the suffering he will endure for all God's people.

Not my will be done, but yours, Lord.

Luke 11. 14–28

The psychology of demons and their casting out is a delicate issue. Jesus is adamant that it is God who casts out demons. Demons are persistent and need guarding against (v. 27). This is an isolated and memorable saying of Jesus'.

'Be sober, be vigilant; because your adversary the devil, as a roaring lion, walketh about, seeking whom he may devour' (1 Pet. 5.8, AV).

Lent

Ash Wednesday morning

Daniel 9. 3–19

The fundamental idea of our dependence on God enters into, and shapes, Daniel's prayer:

Lord, hear; Lord, forgive; Lord, listen and act; God, for your own sake do not delay, because your city and your people bear your name.

1 Corinthians 9. 24–end

The games would be well known by Corinthian Christians. They were all part of the Greek (the Olympics) and Roman (the Forum and the Stadium) culture. What they knew about physically, they were led to think about in relation to their service to God.

*

Ash Wednesday evening

Amos 5. 6–15

'Hate evil, and love good' (v. 15).

Luke 18. 9–14

The tax-collector's prayer, 'God, have mercy on me, sinner that I am,' has become the basis of the 'Jesus Prayer'.

✠

Thursday morning

Genesis 37. 1–11

Joseph, the favourite son of his father Jacob, a dreamer of dreams, is the subject of fierce jealousy by his brothers. The sheaves in the field of his dreams all bow in homage to the one sheaf, or, as Joseph says, 'my sheaf'.

Hebrews 1. 1–6

Often we ask the question, what does this say about Jesus? This early passage overflows with rich description, each worth a long time pondering. Just one of them, in which the nature of Jesus is described with the image of light:

'He is the radiance of God's glory' (v. 3).

Lord, you contain the universe, and I pray that you may contain, surround, embrace me too.

*

Thursday evening

Jeremiah 26. 1–9

The strong and critical words of prophecy are now arousing a physical response from the priests, the prophets and the people (v. 8). They seize Jeremiah, as they were to seize Jesus.

Luke 11. 29–36

Signs and seeing: the people demand an easy and obvious warning and explanation. Jesus points them to their scriptures, and the signs are all there. People can be signs, and the more light they radiate, the clearer the sign. The body full of light is a resurrection body, the glorious body.

Lighten my darkness, Lord, I pray.

Friday morning

Genesis 37. 12–28

At the centre of all the jagged comings and goings of Joseph's brothers, the merchants, and the mediating Reuben, lies the essential act of violence of putting Joseph in a dry cistern.

Hebrews 2. 1–4

Deliver us from evil.
Free us from the bonds that tie us.
Let us not ignore the freedom
that we have held out to us, in your love.

Friday evening

Jeremiah 26. 10–end

If Jeremiah follows the plight of other prophets, then he will not save his life; but he has a friend in Court, Ahikam, son of Shaphan. Prophecy is a dangerous business.

Luke 11. 37–44

Hypocrisy – seeming one thing and being another – receives an 'Alas!' from Jesus, who would have people experience a wholeness of outer and inner, so the fruit and the tree partake of the same richness.

Saturday morning

Genesis 37. 29–end

The cruel trick of dipping Joseph's coat in goat's blood leads Jacob into despair. Joseph is sold into slavery to Potiphar (for four pieces of silver, according to the Talmud).

Hebrews 2. 5–13

It is remarkable what the early Christians made of Jesus, the carpenter's son from Nazareth, as they evaluated his relationship with God. Then they taught it, and worshipped through the words which their experience had made real.

*

Saturday evening

Jeremiah 27. 2, 12–end

The wearing of the yoke was one of Jeremiah's famous prophetic acts. It must really have sunk into the mind and memory of Jerusalem. 'Submit to the yoke of Babylon and you will be saved.'

Luke 11. 45–end

'This generation' had a particular importance for Jesus: upon them depended the attitude of God towards the whole, and thus the urgency and serious intent, and in Matthew's Gospel, the strong sense of judgement on the Pharisees.

✠

WEEKDAYS FOLLOWING THE FIRST SUNDAY OF LENT

Monday morning

Genesis 39. 1–6

Joseph sheds blessings around by his mere presence, and he is gracious in body as well as in spirit.

Hebrews 2. 14–end

It has always been very important to feel that human suffering has been experienced by Jesus, so that his help comes from a sense of unity with us, and that this is communicated in a direct, ordinary and human way.

*

Monday evening

Jeremiah 28

Who is right? In this contest between Jeremiah and Hananiah from Gibeon, Jeremiah prophesies Hananiah's doom, and certainly Hananiah dies.

'If a prophet foretells prosperity, it will be known that the Lord has sent him only when his words come true' (v. 9).

Luke 12. 1–12

Incredibly sharp and original sayings are these by Jesus on a variety of matters, which are likely to confront his disciples after his death: Who will be on my side? What shall I say in public? How do I cope with physical brutality?

O God, who cares for the sparrows, I know you care for me too.

✠

Tuesday morning

Genesis 39. 7–end

The temptations of Joseph by Potiphar's wife (called Zelicha in the Talmud) leave him innocent, but accused.

'But the Lord was with Joseph' (v. 21).

Hebrews 3. 1–6

The image of the household, and family, in which Jesus is the founder and Son of the house, and Moses is the servant, is not as familiar as the body image, but is a helpful and evocative one.

*

Tuesday evening

Jeremiah 29. 1–14

Jeremiah's letter sets out his advice for the exiles, and gives them hope for a return after seventy years.

Luke 12. 13–21

'This night I must surrender my life.'

Lord, help me to hold lightly to my possessions.

✠

Wednesday morning

Genesis 40. 1–15

The King's cup-bearer tells his dream to Joseph.

'All interpretation belongs to God' (v. 8).

Hebrews 3. 7–15

'Today if ye will hear his voice, harden not your hearts' (vv. 7–8, AV). The very thought that 'today' I might hear the voice of God, makes my prayer:

Let me hear, let me receive, your word, today.

*

Wednesday evening

Jeremiah 30. 1–11

'But do not be afraid, Jacob my servant; Israel, do not despair, says the Lord' (v. 10).

Luke 12. 22–34

How easy to be so familiar with a passage like this and no longer to read it so that it impinges on our lives. It is beautiful – the lilies and the ravens, the life free from anxiety about what we cannot change – but it is a very tough option indeed. The joy of this faith, St Francis of Assisi knew.

'God feeds them ...'

✠

Thursday morning

Genesis 40. 16–end

Two women were grinding at the mill: one was taken, the other left; two thieves on Calvary: one was saved, the other was not; two officials: the cup-bearer is saved, the baker is doomed. The divide is a common theme of judgement stories, and the story method, or their shape, does not allow for any blurred edges.

Lord, help me to be on the side of faith rather than doubt, of repentance rather than hardness of heart, on the side of your grace rather than your judgement.

Hebrews 4. 1–10

The concept of the rest is important here: the Sabbath rest we are familiar with; entering into that rest is the great reward of faith. Rest is the space God leaves for standing back from his creation. Rest lets God be God.

*

Thursday evening

Jeremiah 30. 12–22

The wound will be healed and new skin will grow. The city will be rebuilt (Coventry and Dresden); and, in a Messianic prediction, 'one of themselves' will open up access to God.

Luke 12. 35–40

The imminence of the end, in a Gospel which is often reconciled to a longer wait, and the importance of the quality of waiting, are strong here. The bridegroom takes an important part as the image of the returning Son of Man.

Lord, help us to be ready for action, with our lamps lit.

Friday morning

Genesis 41. 1–8, 25–41

Pharaoh's dream is interpreted by Joseph who sees ahead the seven fruitful and the seven lean harvests. As a result of this Joseph gains authority over the whole land of Egypt.

Hebrews 4. 11–end

The word of God is given one of the most memorable images in the Bible: a two-edged sword cutting to the bone's marrow. On another matter, Jesus the High Priest gives to the Torah and the priesthood their new Christian clothes.

*

Friday evening

Jeremiah 31. 1–14

The anthology provenance of Jeremiah becomes clearer here. As a hymn book will have sections on praise, and sections on lament or sorrow, so the Book of Jeremiah seems to be built up in the same way. It is only marginally chronological, but rather, thematic and liturgical.

'Girls will then dance for joy' (v. 13).

Luke 12. 41–48

If waiting for the end were not a problem, then it would have been unlikely that sayings on the subject would be remembered. For us, two millennia on, the urgency becomes a spiritual urgency.

✠

Saturday morning

Genesis 41.55 – 42.17

Joseph, knowing that it is his brothers who have come for the grain, waits to see Benjamin who has remained behind with his father, Jacob.

Hebrews 5

The nature of Christ's priesthood is given more attention.

'Son though he was, he learned obedience through his sufferings' (v. 8).

*

Saturday evening

Jeremiah 31. 15–22

The people are being called back from exile, and for the journey, cairns will be built along the way, as markers for those who follow.

Luke 12. 49–end

The 'hard' sayings of Jesus, full of fire, and uncompromising urgency, are an integral part of any committed life. There will be moments of fire, and long periods of aridity.

WEEKDAYS FOLLOWING THE SECOND SUNDAY OF LENT

Monday morning

Genesis 42. 18–end

'What is this that God has done to us?' (v. 28) With a general sense of things going wrong, in need of reconciling and smoothing out, the chapter sets up a longing for the family to be brought back into unity; if not, 'then shall ye bring down my [Jacob's] gray hairs with sorrow to the grave' (v. 38, AV).

Lord, help us to reconcile our families, our church and our nation.

Hebrews 6. 1–8

Religious experience is the motive for maintaining and deepening the relationship with God. It is like good and creative soil.

'... And some of the seed fell into good soil' (Mark 4. 8).

*

Monday evening

Jeremiah 31. 27–34

At some points in scripture it is possible to see quantum leaps in understanding, and this is one of them: the responsibility of a person for their own behaviour, based on a covenant by God with people in their heart.

Luke 13. 1–9

Some sayings of Jesus are very hard, and there are dark sayings, bleak in their judgements. The common-sense decision to wait for judgement is the way of the Galilean teacher.

✠

Tuesday morning

Genesis 43. 1–15

Jacob's advice, in the end, is full of goodness, wisdom and generosity. 'May God Almighty make him kindly disposed to you.' The calming and righting power of God is called into a difficult situation.

Hebrews 6. 10–end

Those moving in a world of oaths would be no strangers to this passage. The thrust of it is that God will not play us false. Our hope is an anchor.

'Crosses grow Anchors; Bear, as thou shouldst do
Thy Crosse, and that Crosse growes an Anchor too.
But he that makes our Crosses Anchors thus,
Is Christ, who there is crucifi'd for us.'
(John Donne, 'To Mr George Herbert, with one of my Seals')

*

Tuesday evening

Jeremiah 31. 35–end

Such familiar and loving attention to the names of the parts of Jerusalem: and all will be holy to the Lord.

'Make the circuit of Zion; walk round about her;
count the number of her towers' (Ps. 48.11).

Luke 13. 10–17

The authority of Jesus to teach has added cause for criticism, from the president of the synagogue, because of its being on the Sabbath. Doing good is more important in Jesus' eyes than keeping the Sabbath rules.

Wednesday morning

Genesis 43. 16–end

The tension mounts as Benjamin draws near to Joseph, and Joseph's tears begin to shake his stern exterior.

Hebrews 7. 1–14

Melek ('King') Zedek ('righteousness'), King of Salem ('peace'), is a figure who always seems a thousand years old, like Methuselah. He blessed Abram and was a prototype of Christ. Hebrews is as Jewish a writing as Matthew's Gospel.

Wednesday evening

Jeremiah 32. 1–15

The prophetic act, showing confidence in the Lord's promise to bring the people back, is to put down a payment on a piece of land. The field, at poor Anathoth, was the birth-place of Jeremiah, and it had a desolate view of the Dead Sea.

Luke 13. 18–30

What is the Kingdom of God like? It will be a surprise, and the way is narrow.

'Some who are now last will be first,
and some who are first will be last' (v. 30).

✠

Thursday morning

Genesis 44. 1–17

The silver cup is hidden in the bag of the youngest brother. The testing Lord is again making frightening demands of faith. They will have to go home without Benjamin.

Lord, you test us in very difficult ways. Give us the strength we need to remain faithful in the darkness.

Hebrews 7. 15–end

Jesus is the high priest whose one perfect sacrifice atones for our sins, 'superceding the law'.

Lord, you are perfect for ever.

*

Thursday evening

Jeremiah 33. 1–16

Images of judgement are set side by side with images of blessing. God hides his face because of the sin of his people, and then in time of restoration, 'flocks will once more pass under the shepherd's hand as he counts them'.

Good Shepherd, I feel your hand on my head, as one of your flock. May our city be in receipt of your blessings.

Luke 13. 31–end

There is something vividly autobiographical about these lines: 'Go and tell that fox!' and 'O Jerusalem, Jerusalem'. Jesus sees himself in the prophet's role, and is deeply distressed by the Temple, forsaken by God.

✠

Friday morning

Genesis 44. 18–end

Judah pleads that Benjamin should return with the party to Jacob. He knows that it will kill Jacob not to have Benjamin back.

Hebrews 8. 1–6

Jesus is the minister in the real sanctuary. It is he who does the work. We, as earthly ministers, depend entirely on him. He is the mediator between us and the God of a new covenant.

*

Friday evening

Jeremiah 34. 1–7

There can be no more difficult prophecy than to be honest about the defeat and death of a king. Jeremiah had no qualms about telling such truth.

Luke 14. 1–6

This is a Sabbath conflict story in which Jesus asks the question: 'Is it permitted to heal people on the sabbath or not?' Dropsy (Greek *hudropikos*) is internal water: 'swollen with dropsy'. Picture the man. Picture Jesus the healer.

✠

Saturday morning

Genesis 45. 1–15

At last, Joseph's emotions are released and the secret is revealed. Joseph acknowledges that it was God's will that he was sold into Egypt, and seems at this stage to bear no grudge.

Hebrews 8. 6–end

The new covenant:
'This is my blood of the new covenant,
which is shed for you and for many for the
forgiveness of sins' (ASB).

*

Saturday evening

Jeremiah 34. 8–end

A great charter for Hebrew slaves is proclaimed but then gone back on. So the Lord proclaims an ironic deliverance – not from, but into, destruction.

Lord of freedom, who brought your people out of Egypt, free us from the sins that this Lent has brought to mind.

Luke 14. 7–14

If humility is 'endless', in T. S. Eliot's phrase, it must lead into the eternal, and thus be the closest thing to God – self-exaltation being the furthest.

✠

WEEKDAYS FOLLOWING THE THIRD SUNDAY OF LENT

Monday morning

Genesis 45. 16–end

There is something of the Prodigal Son's return in Jacob's response to the news of his son Joseph's whereabouts. Events seem to be leading to a satisfactory conclusion, but over it all hangs our knowledge of the slavery of God's people in Egypt.

'It is enough! Joseph my son is still alive' (v. 28).

Hebrews 9. 1–10

Does the author describe all this because his readers know the facts, but not the full significance of what they know; or is he describing it because they don't know, and need to know; or is he addressing the nominal Jews who might be susceptible to the new covenant, and to Jesus, its mediator?

Jesus, liberator from sins committed, turn me, forgive me, release me.

*

Monday evening

Jeremiah 36. 1–19

The Temple was the place where the prophet would speak the words he had received from God – the sermon writ large. Here is a sermon on petitioning the Lord for forgiveness. Jeremiah is burning to speak.

Lord, help me to know and to say what burns within me.

Luke 14. 15–24

This gospel will not go away: the gospel to the poor, and the gospel to that within us which would like to forget the poor, the sick, the lame, and the blind – who were Jesus' first loves.

✠

Tuesday morning

Genesis 46. 1–7, 28–end

This is the most amazing story. The wonderful climax of meetings is here, that of father and lost son. 'Joseph … wept on his shoulder for a long time.' We have simply to stand around and wait, and let them have their reconciliation. There is no breaking in on this.

Hebrews 9. 11–14

There is some dispute as to whether this Jewish and Temple imagery works, outside of a deep involvement in the Jewish sacrificial system; but blood is surely a universal symbol for both life and death. It is the basic thing.

'But now Christ has come …' (v. 11).

*

Tuesday evening

Jeremiah 36. 20–end

What a tedious and soul-destroying business it must have been to rewrite the scroll after the first had been cut into strips and burned by King Jehoiakim of Judah.

Luke 14. 25–end

There are so many references to the need for poverty and standing loosely to the things of this world, that they build up an authentic picture of sacrificial commitment.

Lord, help me to be prepared to leave all my possessions behind, in order to be your disciple.

✠

Wednesday morning

Genesis 47. 13–end

The famine exacts its toll in financial terms. Joseph increases in power, as does Pharaoh, but the people become slaves of Pharaoh. Jacob dies. He requests his body to be taken to lie with his forebears.

Hebrews 9. 15–end

Thinking of blood – thinking of war, operations, AIDS, transfusions, accidents – makes us realize how crucial an image blood is: sacrifice, and the Eucharist, and George Herbert's 'Christ-side-piercing spear'.

'Without the shedding of blood there is no forgiveness' (v. 22).

*

Wednesday evening

Jeremiah 37. 1–10

The Egyptians are a glimmering hope on the horizon for Jerusalem – but no, the Chaldeans remain a major threat to the security of the city. Jeremiah knows this and gives no military or worldly hope to King Zedekiah. No false hope: that is Jeremiah's strength.

Luke 15. 1–10

The sinner who repents is the one who formerly missed God, and who now hits the mark. Some see the distinction so clearly between the sinner and the saved; others live with shades of grey. Rejoicing *over* the found, week by week, we rejoice *with* the found, of whom we are one.

Thanks be to God.

Thursday morning

Genesis 49.28 – 50.14

The journey to and from Canaan and Egypt seems to be managed without too much difficulty. The Exodus was altogether more lengthy. The death of Jacob/Israel is described so domestically and pragmatically: 'he drew up his feet on to the bed'.

Hebrews 10. 1–10

The many of the former covenant give way to the one of the new. All sacrifices are subsumed into the one offering on the cross.

'... the offering of the body of Jesus Christ, once for all ...' (BCP)

*

Thursday evening

Jeremiah 37. 11–end

Jeremiah has an ambivalent relationship with Zedekiah. He prophesies what Zedekiah doesn't want to hear, and yet demands sanctuary from the dangers of Jonathan the scribe. Jeremiah is given his daily bread from 'Baker Street'.

Luke 15. 11–end

There is again a story of return and restoration over one sinner who repents; or the 'turning' process with its important opportunity to rejoice.

I will rejoice and give thanks to the Lord.

Friday morning

Genesis 50. 15–end

The end of Joseph's life is full of reconciliation and greater understanding of the purposes of God through difficult times.

Hebrews 10. 11–18

The writer presses home the significance of Christ in his role as the true and only High Priest. Priests often assume a great personal significance, but we must point to Christ. Holy Spirit and Word here assume one breath.

*

Friday evening

Jeremiah 38. 1–13

Jeremiah is put in the well, but then pulled out with old clothes tied together. Zedekiah seems to have little power or authority left.

Luke 16. 1–9

This is a notoriously difficult passage, because it seems to advocate dishonesty. Salvaging a meaning from it usually involves praising a strategy which, under the circumstances of the end, leaves a person wise through perceiving the ways of the world. As a result, they are ready for the crisis.

✠

Saturday morning

Exodus 1. 1–14, 22

The sacred historian sees the new regime in power over Egypt, a Pharaoh who did not know Joseph, and the oppression beginning. The Hebrews are set to work, and so it is ironic that the order comes for all the male Hebrew babies to be drowned in the Nile.

Hebrews 10. 19–25

Christ is the model priest, and the congregations need to hold their faith firm, 'for the giver of the promise is to be trusted'.

George Herbert's poem collection *The Temple* has echoes of Hebrews, and begins with a verse from Psalm 29.

'And in the temple of the Lord
all are crying "Glory!" ' (Ps. 29.9)

*

Saturday evening

Jeremiah 38. 14–end
(Scene: the court of the guardhouse)

Zedekiah: Hide nothing from me.
Jeremiah: If I speak out, you will certainly put me to death; if I offer advice you will disregard it.

Compare Jesus before Pilate, Luke 22.67.

Luke 16. 10–15

A series of three sayings on the subject of money and its dangers which shifts in tone quite a lot, from 'You cannot serve God and Money' to 'if you have not proved trustworthy with the wealth of this world …' Money as a symbol of worth stands in the way of God, who is alone worthy of worship.

WEEKDAYS FOLLOWING THE FOURTH SUNDAY OF LENT

Monday morning

Exodus 2. 1–15

There is a divinity breathing through the story of Moses' birth. Pharaoh's daughter was 'moved with pity' for the baby among the reeds. The jump from birth narrative to an account of the adult life of Moses is as rapid as the Gospel account of the same period.

Hebrews 10. 32–end

The central thrust of this letter is to maintain the faith of the people to which it is addressed. It was a faith which held them through suffering and now must continue to do so.

'... the earnest tone of the practical exhortations ... expresses very distinctly the writer's fear that those whom he is addressing are likely to become apostates from the faith of Christ.'

(F. D. Maurice, *Lectures on the Epistle to the Hebrews*)

*

Monday evening

Jeremiah 39. 1–10

After 9 years 10 months of Zedekiah's reign the siege begins. After 11 years 10 months it ends, in victory over Jerusalem by Nebuchadrezzar. Zedekiah, against the advice of Jeremiah, flees, and is captured; and the dreadful prophecy is fulfilled.

Luke 16. 16–18

The three unrelated topics could come under the heading 'Miscellaneous'. Each in its own way is all-important, but Luke does not flesh them out with story or comment.

Tuesday morning

Exodus 3. 1–20

The future escape into freedom is anticipated, and is prepared for by Moses' seeing the eternal glory of God in the burning bush – burning but not burnt up. He also hears the name of God, which is both historical and ever-present. God is both of now, and the God of Abraham, Isaac, and Jacob.

Glory to the Father, and to the Son, and to the Holy Spirit: as it was in the beginning, is now, and shall be for ever. Amen.

Hebrews 11. 1–7

This history is the story, or stories, of faith: here, Abel, Enoch, and Noah. Faith is faith in things unseen.

Lord, teach us to breathe deeply in faith (S. Kierkegaard).

*

Tuesday evening

Jeremiah 39. 11–end

Despite the desperate plight of the city, Jeremiah will not 'fall a victim to the sword', because he trusted in God.

Luke 16. 19–end

Luke's priority for the poor must reflect Jesus' priority for the poor. The rich will have a very difficult time of it at death. The Kingdom theme is absent from the story.

'Dogs used to come and lick his sores.' Who else but Luke would have found room for such detail?

Wednesday morning

Exodus 4. 1–20

Moses needs a considerable amount of persuading by God to fulfil the command to go to Pharaoh and ask for the release of the Hebrews. He feels unworthy.

Lord help me overcome my anxieties and my inadequacies.

Hebrews 11. 8–16

The story of faith continues with Abraham and Sarah. It is a journey story which contains a longing for a better country, and exists as a reward for faith in God.

'My soul, there is a country
Far beyond the stars ...'

(Henry Vaughan, 'Peace')

*

Wednesday evening

Jeremiah 40. 1–6

The Exile is beginning and Jeremiah is given the choice, whether or not to go into exile. He chooses to go to Mizpah, north of Jerusalem, to stay with Gedaliah, who has been put in charge of the remaining Jews.

'Where can I flee from your presence?' (Ps. 139.6)

Luke 17. 1–10

Some instruction for the disciples on general matters: but each takes us far out of the general run of ethical duty into supernatural love, endless forgiveness, and not asking for any reward.

Teach us, O Lord, to give and not to count the cost.

✠

Thursday morning

Exodus 5. 1–14, 22–end

The battle lines are beginning to be drawn, between Pharaoh's greed for more work from the workforce, and the Israelites who want to worship the Lord, their God. Moses stands between the two.

Hebrews 11. 17–22

Abraham and Isaac, Isaac and Jacob, Jacob and Joseph: the torch of faith is handed on.

*

Thursday evening

Jeremiah 40. 7–end

Gedeliah gathers round himself at Mizpah a great many Hebrews, and rumours of the plot to assassinate him are heard, but not heeded.

Luke 17. 11–19

It is the most unexpected one who finds favour with God, and who returns not just for healing, but for wholeness of life.

'One … turned back with shouts of praise to God' (v. 15).

Friday morning

Exodus 6. 2–13; 7. 1–7

God asserts his power over events – as Lord, as well as the traditional God of the forebears. Moses, bemused and feeling inadequate, is both receiver and communicator of the word of the Lord.

God of the past, Lord of the present,
lead us into your future.

Hebrews 11. 23–31

Moses is remembered in the tradition by his particular acts of faith. Can we imagine this whole list sung as a litany in the worship of the Early Church, or is it too much of a prose work?

Lord, if it be your will, give us a faith that helps a whole people.

✳

Friday evening

Jeremiah 41. 1–10

Ishmael's depravity is mean and sordid and full of duplicity. It obviously scarred the memory of the Judaeans. King Asa's Well stands alongside Auschwitz as a monument to evil.

Luke 17. 20–end

The Kingdom is not a matter of observation. It will come from God in God's good time. It will be divisive – 'one will be taken, the other left' – and a complete surprise. So, be ready.

✠

Saturday morning

Exodus 7. 8–end

A test of power leaves Pharaoh 'obdurate', despite the turning of Aaron's staff into a snake and the River Nile into blood.

Hebrews 11. 32–end

Receiving back the dead raised to life, and winning a resurrection to a better life, are nicely distinguished by the author. All the heroes of faith under the old covenant wait to be perfected with those of the new.

✳

Saturday evening

Jeremiah 41. 11–end

Johanan, son of Kareah, is the great hero who comes to defeat Ishmael. Ishmael slips through the net, but his former prisoners are full of relief.

'I the Lord have called you with righteous purpose … to bring captives out of prison' (Isa. 42. 6, 7).

Luke 18. 1–8

The importunate widow is an all-too-human example of someone who gets their way through persistence. If this can happen in the world, how much more will God listen and act. More important is whether the Son of Man will find faith when he comes.

'… Ever faithful, ever sure' (H. W. Baker).

Passiontide

WEEKDAYS FOLLOWING THE FIFTH SUNDAY OF LENT

Monday morning

Exodus 8. 1–15

There is a regular formula for describing the plagues: the Lord to Moses, Moses to Pharaoh, the Lord to Moses and Aaron, Pharaoh to Moses and Aaron. Moses asks the Lord to stem the plague. He does, but Pharaoh remains obdurate. 'Obdurate' means 'hard-hearted'.

Hebrews 12. 1–11

The 'great cloud of witnesses' are always such a comfort in an empty church, or under difficulty and hardship; but above all, we think of Christ. The place of discipline, unfashionable though it is, sets us on the path of life.

*

Monday evening

Jeremiah 42. 1–6

O Lord, which way are we to take and what are we to do? Tell us and we will do it, so that it will go well with us, through our obedience to you.

Luke 18. 9–14

God have mercy on me,
sinner that I am.

✠

Tuesday morning

Exodus 8. 16–end

… maggots, flies … A three days' journey into the wilderness to intercede is an early example of a spiritual discipline.

Hebrews 12. 12–22

Mount Sinai, the terrifying old covenant, is contrasted with Mount Zion, the city of the living God, the heavenly Jerusalem (v. 22).

*

Tuesday evening

Jeremiah 42. 7–17

Jeremiah hears from the Lord the command that people should stay where they are. Going into Egypt would be both disobedience and courting disaster.

Teach us, Lord, to sit still.

Luke 18. 15–17

What quality in children is Jesus talking about, when he says we must possess it to enter the Kingdom? The desire to be in there, close to Jesus himself – their unstoppability, if that is a word.

✠

Wednesday morning

Exodus 9. 1–12

... pestilence, boils ... We wonder how God has it in him to inflict disasters such as these; but looked at in the light of the whole purpose of God, which is to free his people, it begins to be comprehensible. We begin to see the way they thought.

'God so loved the world that he gave his only Son' (John 3.16).

Hebrews 12. 25–end

The 'oracle' is an oblique reference to some sort of response. The author here makes a distinction between human advice (Moses' perhaps) and the real things (God's word in Jesus).

Lord, let us worship you, as you would be worshipped.

Wednesday evening

Jeremiah 42. 18–end

Those who are intending to go to Egypt are severely warned by Jeremiah. Always the firm voice, never any sense of 'perhaps'.

Luke 18. 18–30

This is one of those piercing passages which go the heart, here addressed to a rich young man. Jesus spots, like a hawk, the things that block out a true love of God.

Lord, what is impossible for us, is possible for you. Help me to do impossible things.

Thursday morning

Exodus 9. 13–end

… hailstorm … Moses 'lifted up his hands to the Lord in prayer'. Pharaoh remained obdurate.

Hebrews 13. 1–6

Some duties are described here which we would do well to pin on our walls: be hospitable, honour marriage, do not live for money.

*

Thursday evening

Jeremiah 43

I had never envisaged Jeremiah going into Egypt, harrying the Judaeans who went there, and saying that Nebuchadrezzar would destroy their part of Egypt too. Was this an imaginary appearance or a real one?

Luke 18. 31–end

The age of the prophets and the fulfilment of their words reach their climax in the death and resurrection of Jesus. The blind will soon see, and understand, this.

Friday morning

Exodus 10. 1–11

The Lord's method – reminiscent of parts of John's Gospel – where he makes Pharaoh obdurate, so that he may show signs, seems a strange method to us. Locusts are threatened, and so the signs go on.

Hebrews 13. 7–16

Jesus is the same, yesterday, today and for ever, and yet he is also the human body of God who suffered outside the gate.

'There is a green hill far away
without a city wall' (C. F. Alexander).

*

Friday evening

Jeremiah 44. 1–14

'You shall have no other gods before me' (Exod. 20.3, NIV). This commandment was broken in Judah, and is now being broken in Egypt among the Judaeans in exile. The oneness of God is central to Jewish faith.

Luke 19. 1–10

Luke is the master of brevity: everything that needs to be said is said, nothing is missing. Jesus goes after Zacchaeus, like the shepherd after the lost sheep.

✠

Saturday morning

Exodus 10. 12–end

… locusts, darkness … The extent of this section on the plagues makes me wonder how it was originally used. Perhaps it was used dramatically. There is a ritual quality to it which repetitively expresses the struggle to find freedom.

'Let my people go.'

Hebrews 13. 17–21

Some simple, straightforward advice is concluded by the great, and model, blessing:

May the God of peace … make you perfect in all goodness.

*

Saturday evening

Jeremiah 45

Jeremiah writes to Baruch at Baruch's own dictation, which seems a little strange. Baruch, as he wrote, must have felt his heart sinking, but eventually he was cheered by the fact that his life would be saved.

'The Lord has punished me sorely,
but he did not hand me over to death'
(Ps. 118.18).

Luke 19. 11–27

Some historical echoes rebound here: the unpopular appointment of Archelaus as King of Judea in 4 BC (v. 14), and the mass execution of AD 70 (v. 27). God cannot latch on to a blank surface – that is the 'nothing' that will be forfeited – but the slightest glimmer of faith will attach to itself even more.

O Lord, by grace, may I be saved through faith (Eph. 2.8).

WEEKDAYS IN HOLY WEEK

Monday morning

Lamentations 1. 1–12a

Jerusalem suffers in her feminine character: widowed, betrayed, mocked, and naked.

'Is it nothing to you, all you who pass by?' (v. 12, NIV)

John 14

Father, Son, and Holy Spirit interact to provide direction ('I am the way'), and comfort ('Set your troubled hearts at rest'), in these final days.

*

Monday evening

Lamentations 2. 8–19

If we place this now, we might find some similar tragic scenes:

'Must women eat the fruit of their wombs,
the children they have held in their arms?
Should priest and prophet be slain
in the sanctuary of the Lord?' (v. 20)

Year A *Colossians 1. 18–23*

The universal dimension of the cross is revealed. Jesus reconciled all things, both in heaven and earth.

Year B *1 Peter 2. 19–end*

Christ's death is both an example for us, and through his sinless death cancels our sins, and leads us into a godly life.

Year C *Hebrews 2. 9–end*

The cross is a battle with the devil, a sacrifice for sin, and a means of empathizing with our situation of suffering.

✠

Tuesday morning

Lamentations 3. 1–18 (19–30)

This autobiography of suffering is one in which the Lord causes the suffering:

'Even when I cry out and plead for help
he rejects my prayer' (v. 8).

John 15.1 – 16.4a

The vine, and the word, and the love, are the three great elements of the Eucharist.

*

Tuesday evening

Lamentations 3. 40–51

God is a hidden God.

'You have covered yourself with a cloud beyond reach of our prayers' (v. 44).

*

Tuesday evening

Year A *Galatians 6. 11–end*

The cross is a way of dying to the world and its superficial values epitomized in the rite of circumcision. Paul bears the marks of Christ in his body. The stigmata are his circumcision.

Year B *Philippians 3. 7–11*

The way to resurrection glory has to be, with Christ, through suffering.

Year C *Hebrews 9. 15–end*

The Jews understood sacrifice as a concept for dealing with sin. The Letter to Hebrews claims Christ as the one and only complete sacrifice for the sins of the whole world.

✠

Wednesday morning

Wisdom 1.16 – 2. 1, 12–22

The questioners are first-century Alexandrians jeering at holiness as the bystanders jeered at Jesus on the cross, but holiness has its recompense.

Let us bless the Lord.

or Jeremiah 11. 18–20

Jeremiah, speaking out of his own heart, touched Jesus' heart and now ours. Christ took on the prophetic role of 'pet lamb led to the slaughter' but with no hint of revenge.

John 16. 4b–end

The crucifixion is a going, or return, for Jesus the Son, to the Father ('He was in the beginning' with God at John 1.2). So it is a homecoming. The disciples will then have a beloved Lord at the right hand of the Father, and contact through the Holy Spirit. They – we – have no need for fear, or trouble, or worry.

*

Wednesday evening

Isaiah 63. 1–9

Treading the wine-press alone, and staining the garments red, evoke the crucifixion, and the true vine, and the washing in the blood of the Lamb:

'It is I, proclaiming a victory.
I, who am strong to save' (v. 1).

Year A *Ephesians 2. 11–18*

Christ has opened a door by his death, through which all can go to be at one, and in peace, with God.

Year B *Romans 5. 6–19*

Jesus' death on the cross was a proof of God's love for us, despite our abject failure and sin: and thus salvation, and exultation, and reconciliation.

Alleluia!

Year C *Hebrews 10. 1–10*

Here I am, says Jesus, I am the sacrifice, to put an end to all ineffectual sacrifices.

'I have come, O God, to do your will.'

✠

Maundy Thursday morning

Leviticus 16. 2–24

The protocol of offerings for priest and people – bulls and goats, to make 'expiation' – reflect a longing in people to be right with God. Against this background we set the cross of Christ, with its own brutal and tragic protocol.

John 17

Looking out from his own relationship to the Father, Jesus contemplates his disciples and the people who believe in him. The Trinity is not a closed circuit: it generates love, and receives love.

*

Thursday evening

Exodus 11

The 'great cry, the like of which has never been heard before, nor ever will be again', hangs like a great question mark over the purpose of God at this point. It is freedom at a great cost. We think of the cost of the cross of Christ, and see love, and not carnage.

'One person should die for the people' (John 11.50).

Year A *Luke 22. 7–30*

The Last Supper is full of emotion for all: for Jesus because it is his last; Judas for his betrayal of Jesus; the disciples over their anxiety about leadership and status.

'This is my body.'

Year B *Matthew 26. 17–29*

The severity of Judas' imminent betrayal of Jesus dominates Matthew's account of the Last Supper.

'This is my blood, the blood of the covenant, shed for many.'

Year C *Mark 14. 12–25*

Jesus had it all arranged, in secrecy: the man with the jar of water, the householder, the room set out in readiness:

'Never again shall I drink from the fruit of the vine until that day when I drink it new in the kingdom of God.'

✠

Good Friday morning

Genesis 22. 1–18

Wood for the sacrifice, a climb up a hill, the carrying of the wood on the shoulders of the son – the father and his only son – and then 'Stop!' The cross was not yet. God waited.

Year A *Luke 22.66 – 23.49*

'Father, forgive them.'

'Today you will be with me in Paradise.'

Year B *Matthew 27. 1–54*

'This is Jesus, the king of the Jews.'

'He saved others, but he cannot save himself.'

Year C *Mark 15. 1–39*

'Eloï, Eloï, lema sabachthani?'

'My God, my God, why have you forsaken me?'

*

Friday evening

Lamentations 5. 15–end

The body is in the tomb. All is quiet now, with a tiredness of body and spirit. A sense that we did not do enough.

'Mount Zion is desolate
and overrun with jackals' (v. 18).

Hebrews 4. 14–16; 5. 7–9

At this very time, Christ is 'passing through the heavens', having lived a fully human life, and soon he will call us to be with him.

Hebrews 10. 12–22

At the foot of the cross lie our sins, to be forgotten for ever. Thanks be to God.

or Year A *Luke 23. 50–end*

The evening of spices and perfumes, and tears, and a deep silence ...

Year B *Matthew 27. 55–61*

Joseph took the body and wrapped it in a clean linen sheet, and laid it in his own unused tomb. The physicality of it. The closeness to Jesus. As close as anyone, ever.

Year C *Mark 15. 40–end*

Mary of Magdala saw where he was laid: ever vigilant for her beloved Lord.

'Who is this that looks out like the dawn?' (S. of S. 6.10).

Morning of Easter Eve

Job 14. 1–14

'Man that is born of a woman hath but a short time to live.'

At how many blustery gravesides have these words flown away? – but there is a hope in Job, although we rarely read on to the lines:

'I would not lose hope,
however long my service,
waiting for my relief to come.
You would summon me and I would answer'
(vv. 14, 15).

Matthew 27. 62–end

This is the day of the guard, in Matthew, and the sealing of the stone. I see the sleeping soldier and an awakening Christ.

*

Evening of Easter Eve

Job 19. 21–27

'For I know that my redeemer liveth,
and that he shall stand at the latter day
upon the earth ...' (v. 25, AV).

And we shall be close enough to see for ourselves what up to now we have only pictured and dreamed. To see is to know, and to know is to be known, and to be known is to be loved.

1 Peter 3. 18 – 4.6

Christ Jesus, proclaim to my
imprisoned spirit the good
news of your victory
Tell me the waters will subside.

Eastertide

WEEKDAYS FOLLOWING EASTER DAY

Monday morning

Isaiah 25. 1–9

Standing up to bullying nations is one of God's attributes, out of which comes this hymn to joy, a cantata to glory.

O Lord, let us exult and rejoice in your deliverance.

Matthew 28. 1–7

He has been raised, said the angel to the women. The heart that heard it first, and the hand that wrote it first: this is holy ground.

*

Monday evening

Song of Songs 2. 8–end

God said to his beloved, 'My dove', you are trying so hard to love me, straining so much:

'Let me see your face and hear your voice;
for your voice is sweet, your face is lovely.'

Acts 5. (17–26) 27–32

'The God of our fathers raised up Jesus, after you had put him to death by hanging him on a gibbet' (v. 30). Peter, the one who had denied Jesus, now stands before the high priest and professes his faith.

'I believe in Jesus Christ.'

✠

Tuesday morning

Isaiah 26. 1–19

O Lord,
with all my heart I long for you,
at dawn I seek for you.

John 20. 1–10

There is no angel here, but there is a linking up of what they saw (or did not see, since Jesus was not there), and what they half-remembered from the scriptures about the fact that 'Jesus must rise from the dead'.

*

Tuesday evening

Micah 7. 7–end

Gloating over defeated enemies is still a lingering theme, but it is being replaced by a new hope, forgiveness of sins, and a showing of the mercy of God.

Lord, I will watch for you:
God, my Saviour, I shall wait for you.

Acts 13. 26–41

Paul addressing his 'brothers … of Abraham's stock', recites the credal facts of Jesus' life, death, and resurrection. Their significance is in the forgiveness of sins, which would never have been possible under the law of Moses.

✠

Wednesday morning

Isaiah 42. 10–16

'Sing a new song to the Lord': praise his victory, leading the blind and turning their darkness into light.

Luke 24. 1–12

The angels of God encourage the women out of their fear and disbelief; and they, in turn, have to do the same for the disciples. Jesus is not haunting the place of the dead, but is alive and risen.

Lord, let me not be like those who go down to the Pit.

*

Wednesday evening

Zechariah 3. 14–end

The quality of rejoicing is all the greater when it comes after a time of pain. It brings not cries of woe, but shouts of joy.

Acts 17. 16–31

Paul on the heights commands a panoramic view not only of the Parthenon, but also of much of the pagan world, and speaks about the resurrection, and how it provides assurance for the forgiveness of sins, and the veracity of Jesus as Lord. Of these things he would not have us ignorant.

✠

Thursday morning

Isaiah 43. 16–21

O, all out of love – the pain out of love, and now the joy out of love: 'This people I have formed for myself,' says the Lord. Being loved by God is an adventure which has its heights and depths.

Revelation 1. 4–18

This figure that John sees is a remarkable compilation of biblical images. The feeling is of strength rather than of beauty, complexity not simplicity. It is John's view of the One who rules from the seat of glory.

'I was dead and now I am alive for evermore.'

*

Thursday evening

Jeremiah 31. 1–14

... dancing, planting, eating, gathering, being led home ... heaven on earth: here is a rare diamond in Jeremiah, of the joy of the release from exile.

Revelation 7. 9–end

John reaches into unbelievable heights of praise and thanksgiving, through the intensity of his images, and by setting such great hopes beside such deep suffering.

'They have washed their robes, and made them white in the blood of the Lamb' (v. 14). Revelation is the amen of The Book.

✠

Friday morning

Isaiah 51. 1–11

The writer is working in opposites: wilderness and Eden (v. 3), the temporary and the eternal (v. 6); and out of all the pain and the past will come victory.

1 Corinthians 15. 1–11

The appearances of Christ in the period of the resurrection are what really thrill Paul, and the fact that he was allowed to meet the risen Christ himself.

*

Friday evening

Ezekiel 37. 1–14

'Can these bones live?' is a question that challenges all involved in building communities. What better image of things coming to life after a seemingly sure death?

Lord, help us to see that things grown old are being made new.

Acts 26. 1–23

Paul, before Agrippa and Festus, concludes his '*apologia*' with the idea that the Messiah, as the first to rise from the dead, would announce the dawn to both Jew and Gentile.

'The dawn from on high shall break upon us' (Benedictus).

✠

Saturday morning

Isaiah 61

We can hear Jesus reading this in the synagogue at Nazareth; but rather than bask in its beauty, he used it as an opportunity to begin his work of inaugurating the Kingdom.

Mark 16. 1–8

The famous, abrupt ending of Mark leaves fear or faithlessness as its last word. What do you think is Mark's challenge? Where do you stand? Do you listen and not really hear?

Lord, in the mystery of the cross, let me see your love, and in the mystery of the resurrection let me hear the gospel message again: 'Repent and believe.'

Saturday evening

Zechariah 8. 1–8

The dream of the ordinary people in all the war-torn cities of the world might be:

'Old men and women will sit
in the streets of Jerusalem …
and the streets … will be full
of boys and girls at play' (vv. 4, 5).

'And young men glittering and sparkling Angels, and maids strange seraphic pieces of life and beauty! Boys and girls tumbling in the street, and playing, were moving jewels.'
(Thomas Traherne, *Centuries*)

1 John 5. 4–12

The exclusivity of John (v. 12) is somehow tempered by the graciousness of the Son of God himself, as if the One being written about is, inevitably, more loving than the writing.

WEEKDAYS FOLLOWING THE SECOND SUNDAY OF EASTER

Monday morning

Exodus 16. 2–15

'Bread of heaven,
feed me now and evermore' (W. Williams).

'He rained down manna upon them to eat and gave them grain from heaven' (Ps. 78.24).

Revelation 1. 1–8

The panoply of divinity that surrounds the pierced Jesus is exhilarating, and can be confusing. John is gathering up everything and consciously writing a finale.

*

Monday evening

Deuteronomy 1. 3–18

Law is the atmosphere we breathe in Deuteronomy, 'preached law'; and the concept of law is an exalted one.

'You must be impartial and listen to high and low alike: have no fear of your fellows, for judgement belongs to God' (v. 17).

1 Peter 1. 1–9

'In his great mercy by the resurrection ...': it is out of that great reality, experienced by the disciples, that suffering is overcome by joy.

✠

Tuesday morning

Exodus 17

The 'murmuring' continues (much decried in the Benedictine Rule e.g. chapters 40 and 41), but Moses finds water for his people at the spring of Meribah. Moses, with his arm stretched up to gain a victory, is strongly resonant of Christ on the cross.

'The Lord is my Banner' (v. 15).

Revelation 1. 9–end

A figure is like a man, but a supernatural man, wearing the symbols of power and judgement, and intimately related to the seven churches. His face has the burning gold of the setting sun, shining over the water lapping the island of Patmos.

✳

Tuesday evening

Deuteronomy 4. 1–14

Horeb is the central place, the giving of the law the central act, and the main threat is the worship of foreign idols.

1 Peter 1. 10–12

The place of the writings of the prophets is a crucial factor in the momentum of the gospel. The gospel illuminates the prophets and fulfils the scripture.

✠

Wednesday morning

Exodus 18. 1–12

Jethro, Zipporah, Gershon and Eliezer come to Moses in the desert and there is an emotional family reunion, full of blessings and thanksgivings to God for the way things have gone.

'Blessed be the Lord who has delivered you from the power of Egypt' (v. 10).

Revelation 2. 1–7

The Church at Ephesus: there is praise, and criticism, but the prize is worth all the rest: 'the right to eat from the tree of life that stands in the garden of God'.

Wednesday evening

Deuteronomy 4. 32–40

'All will be well' (v. 40) is a reminder of the use of the phrase by Mother Julian of Norwich, 'all shall be well and all manner of thing shall be well'. The basis for optimism is the presence of God in the burning bush, and in the Exodus from Egypt, and in the keeping of God's law.

1 Peter 1. 13–21

The way to holiness is in our minds and our will, and in acknowledgement of the gift of God, through Christ Jesus.

*

Thursday evening

Exodus 18. 13–end

The Old Testament takes on its strong administrative colourings. Helpers for Moses are needed to organize things and to hear the problems of the law.

'The Lord appointed a further seventy-two' (Luke 10.1).

Revelation 2. 8–11

The Church at Smyrna: The myrrh of suffering has always been associated with Smyrna.

'Be faithful till death, and I will give you the crown of life' (v. 10).

*

Thursday evening

Deuteronomy 6. 4–15

Strict warnings against believing in false gods lead the writer to direct attention to the liberation experienced in the past, and to the glorious hope of a future settlement.

1 Peter 1. 22–end

The gospel is the enduring word.

'My words will never pass away'
(Matt. 24.35).

✠

Friday morning

Exodus 19. 1–15

Sinai rears up, in the imagination, to the clouds of heaven. The holiness of the mountain and the purity of the people are paramount. Some great thing is imminent.

Revelation 2. 12–17

The Church at Pergamum: charting their way into orthodoxy between the Nicolitains and the Balaamites, those who steer successfully will receive a white stone (a stone with Christ's name on it) and the hidden manna (Christ the true manna).

*

Friday evening

Deuteronomy 8. 7–end

A vision of the abundant, natural riches of the Promised Land has attached to it warnings of pride, that the Israelites should not imagine they have done it all themselves. God is their provider.

1 Peter 2. 1–10

'You are living stones': Peter's name means 'stone', or 'rock', built into a spiritual temple, 'stone on stone'.

✠

Saturday morning

Exodus 19. 16–end

A great fear was that the people and the priests would force their way to the Lord, up the holy mountain.

O Lord, you did not grasp at equality with God, but humbled yourself. Help us to imitate your humility.

Revelation 2. 18–end

Authority over the nations and the dawn star will come with victory over the impurities of the cult of Jezebel.

'Blessed are the pure in heart: for they shall see God' (Matt. 5.8, AV).

Saturday evening

Deuteronomy 9. 1–6

'The Lord your God' will secure victory over the giant descendants of Anakim. 'Do not say to yourselves, "It is because of our merits that the Lord has brought us in to occupy this land" ' (v. 4).

1 Peter 2. 11–12

'Avoid bodily desires which make war on the soul'.

My heart, O Lord, is restless until it finds its rest in you.

✠

WEEKDAYS FOLLOWING THE THIRD SUNDAY OF EASTER

Monday morning

Exodus 20. 1–21

Perhaps if we said these commandments more frequently they would have more effect, repetition affecting the deep springs of conduct. Verses 18–21: the fear of God and the dark cloud.

'Covetousness which is idolatry …' (Col. 3.5, RSV).

'… unique in its concentration on what is fundamental and essential' (Martin Noth).

Revelation 3. 1–6

The Church at Sardis: 'Wake up, and put some strength into what you still have, because otherwise it must die!' There will be times when we have to heed this more urgently than at others.

Lord, help us to discern the time.

Monday evening

Deuteronomy 10. 12–end

O Lord God,
to you belongs heaven itself,
the highest heaven,
the earth and everything in it.
I will seek to honour you,
conform to your ways,
love you,
and serve you with all my heart and soul.

1 Peter 2. 13–17

'Submit yourselves' means 'be subject': not unquestioningly, but as Jesus put himself under the obedience of being human and served others.

Grant, Lord, that I may not so much seek to be loved as to love.

Tuesday morning

Exodus 24

Moses is at the heart of all this cultic activity. He performs the ceremonies, and he waits on God. Jesus, as the new Moses, also spent forty days and nights in a remote place.

Revelation 3. 7–13

The Church at Philadelphia: though small they are faithful, and their reward is to know the name and the nature of God.

*

Tuesday evening

Deuteronomy 12. 1–14

A sense here of the 'dangerous holiness' of God, as Martin Noth put it in his commentary on Exodus. Before communicating the Law, Moses prepares himself by time alone with God.

1 Peter 2. 18–end

Peter understands the effective suffering of the cross.

Lord, I thank you that by your wounds I have been healed.

Wednesday morning

Exodus 32. 1–14

The temptation came to the Israelites in the desert while Moses was 'in retreat'. Similarly, at the Mount of Transfiguration, while Jesus was in glory, the disciples were struggling to heal, without success. For the Israelites, the temptation was to idolatry.

Yours, Lord, is the greatness.

Revelation 3. 14–end

The Church at Laodicea: the complaint is that the Christians at Laodicea are neither hot nor cold, but lukewarm, apathetic, perhaps fearful.

Lord, I hear you knocking at the door. I will come and let you in, that we may eat together.

*

Wednesday evening

Deuteronomy 15. 1–18

One way of dealing with poverty in the land is to offer a remission of debt, once every seven years, a jubilee year: practical rules for dealing with common problems. In the same way, slaves are offered remission, unless they are content to remain.

Lord, you show your graciousness most of all in pardoning. Bless us in all we do, if it be your will and your work, and may you be seen in the long-suffering of our hearts.

1 Peter 3. 1–7

Understanding of the role of women in society has changed radically in the west, but the ground rules for marriage have not, and Peter's words (v. 7) still stand:

'[In marriage] God's gift of life is something you share together. Then your prayers will not be impaired.'

✠

Thursday morning

Exodus 32. 15–24, 30

Coming down from the mountain with such high hopes of righteousness in his hands, Moses hears the chaos of idolatry from a long way off.

Grind the false god of my faithlessness, and let me drink it, so that I may repent.

Revelation 4

The vision of heaven is full of colour, and it is circular, and the light of the fire and spirit is caught in the crowns of the elders.

'... the One who sits on the throne ...' (v. 10).

*

Thursday evening

Deuteronomy 16. 1–17

The annual calendar of festivals is Passover (or Unleavened Bread); the pilgrim feast of Weeks and the pilgrim feast of Booths, remembering the hasty flight from Egypt; and two harvest feasts. Rejoicing is an important element in them, although Passover is more sombre.

1 Peter 3. 8–12

Lord, your ears are open to my prayer; help me to respond to abuse with a blessing, and restrain my tongue.

Friday morning

Exodus 33. 7–end

Quite close encounters between Moses and God reveal two different emphases: one of great intimacy, 'face to face', and the other of reticence, distance, and hiddenness.

'Many priests fumble it, for God is unique, better left unnamed than given a name, more unknown than known'.
(Meister Eckhart, *The Sermons*)

Revelation 5

Of all the senses that are here being evoked, it is to the ear that this chapter speaks; but the Lamb, though central, is silent.

*

Friday evening

Deuteronomy 17. 8–end

The process of holding together a community with compassionate love under obedience to the Lord God is seen here in action. The notion of kingship is also seen, but only in embryo.

Lord, let me have your law by me, and help me to read from it all my life.

1 Peter 3. 13–17

The notion of 'martyrdom' is both suffering and witness.

'Hold Christ in your hearts in reverence as Lord' (v. 15).

Saturday morning

Exodus 34. 1–10, 27

Moses meets God in secret on the mountain. No one else must be near. It compares with Jesus' secrecy over his relation to God in Mark's Gospel.

O God, you are compassionate and gracious, long-suffering, ever faithful and true.

Revelation 7. 1–4, 9–end

'Palm branches in their hands': and so began a long tradition of Christian iconography. This is a magisterial picture of the faith of Christians and their destiny. The Lamb becomes the Shepherd, and there is a great paradox in the robes washed in blood being shining white.

*

Saturday evening

Deuteronomy 18. 9–end

The way God communicates with his people is through his chosen prophets. Any other means should be shunned.

Lord, help me to see you in your purity and truth.

1 Peter 3. 18–end

In this credal statement there is crucifixion; baptism, which is salvation through the resurrection of Jesus Christ; and the acknowledgement of Jesus' ascension. Baptism takes a very important place: it is both washing and entry into new life.

✠

WEEKDAYS FOLLOWING THE FOURTH SUNDAY OF EASTER

Monday morning

Exodus 40. 16–21, 34–end

The testimony was covered and covered again. The desire to arch over the holy is a very basic idea. The Lord's holiness covers all in a cloud.

'The testimony of the Lord is sure
and gives wisdom to the innocent' (Ps. 19.7).

Revelation 10. 8–end

The little scroll is open in the hand of the angel who stands on the sea and on the land, and John has to take the scroll and eat it. It is sweet to his mouth, but sour to his stomach. The gospel needs to be proclaimed, it cannot be stored.

*

Monday evening

Deuteronomy 19. 1–13

The cities of sanctuary are quite a sophisticated idea, and are intended for the safety of those who did not kill in a premeditated way. The notion of responsibility is one which is still crucial in matters of life and death.

'Do not commit murder' (Exod. 20.13).

1 Peter 4. 1–6

The spiritual life is so hard. It turns its back on all that leads to death, so that we can live in Christ. '... licence and debauchery' are 'lasciviousness, lusts' in the AV.

✠

Tuesday morning

Leviticus 23. 1, 4–11, 15–16, 27, 34–end

Appointed seasons, ways of remembering, and giving thanks; being sorrowful; and organizing life round religious memories, are all signs of a settled community working its way into an orientation towards God.

Revelation 11. 4–12

Conflict one against another, and in the middle two olive trees and two lamps which stand as symbols of vulnerability: the olive trees reminding us of the Mount of Olives and Jesus in his agony, and the lamp set up as a witness, but exposed to view.

*

Tuesday evening

Deuteronomy 21.22 – 22.8

These are some miscellaneous laws which mainly have a humanitarian emphasis. The attack on cross-dressing is probably in reaction to Canaanite practices.

1 Peter 4. 7–11

The epistle has a great theme of Christian friendliness running through it: 'Be hospitable ... love covers a host of sins.' Christian conduct and personality are important, but deep theological insight, less so.

In all things let God be glorified through Jesus Christ: to him belong glory and praise for ever and ever. Amen.

✠

Wednesday morning

Leviticus 25. 1, 8–17

Land ... land ... to keep sabbaths ... 'It is to be a jubilee year for you: each of you is to return to his holding, everyone to his family' (v. 10). Family and land are very strong ties in this tradition. To celebrate, do we think first of our families? At Christmas we do.

Revelation 11.19 – 12.6

'A woman robed with the sun' is the Blessed Virgin Mary, or any mother about to bear a child, in a world such as ours. God takes the woman up from danger, and places her in the desert for 1260 days.

Good Lord, deliver us.

*

Wednesday evening

Deuteronomy 26. 1–11

Thanksgiving for the fruits of the earth, and for the release from Egypt: both are brought together in this Harvest Festival.

For what we receive, may the Lord make us truly thankful.

1 Peter 4. 12–end

'The sting of death is sin' (1 Cor. 15.56). The writer is conscious of an imminent judgement, which colours the nature of faith and conduct.

I confess the name of Jesus
to the honour of God.

Thursday morning

Numbers 11. 4–15, 30

Moses deals with his grumbling people. This time they are grumbling about food. His 'dealing' consists in an abject cry to God – for help, or an early death.

Revelation 12. 7–12

Blessed be Michael the archangel for taking on the devil and being victorious.

'This is the time of victory for our God, the time of his power and sovereignty, when his Christ comes to his rightful rule.' Only the Easter liturgy could really support such tremendous words, proclaimed in community.

*

Thursday evening

Deuteronomy 28. 58–end

To honour and revere the Lord is the cause of blessing. Not to honour the Lord is to receive his distress.

'Every morning you will say, "Would God it were evening!" and every evening, "Would God it were morning!" ' (v. 67).

1 Peter 5. 1–5

The image of the sheep and the shepherd is a common pastoral one. The underlying motif, though, is that of a 'witness to Christ's sufferings'. By the Gospel accounts, that was for Peter second-hand, since he had deserted Jesus; but it was a crucial experience for all his writings.

Friday morning

Numbers 12. 1–13

The Lord deals with the grumbling of Miriam and Aaron by causing Miriam to have a skin disease, and telling them of Moses' virtues.

'Of all my household he alone is faithful.' This is the God who is intimate with Moses. 'With him I speak face to face, openly and not in riddles' (v. 8).

Lord, may I grow ever closer to you.

Revelation 14. 1–13

St John never fails to bring out the 'shadow' side of the world. He can plumb the depths of human and cosmic evil, as well as raise us to the glorious heights of heaven. Faith is a battleground between good and evil.

'Happy are the dead who henceforth die in the faith of the Lord!' (v. 13).

*

Friday evening

Deuteronomy 29. 1–15

The 'covenant' or agreement between the Lord and his people ...: a promise, a vow, a commitment seem mainly legalistic – there is not a lot of warmth to it; but the passion is coming.

1 Peter 5. 6–end

The exhortation to remain firm in suffering is coloured by the hope of glory.

May the God of our grace, who called you to his eternal glory in Christ, restore, establish, and strengthen you on a firm foundation; for all power belongs to him for ever and ever! Amen.

Saturday morning

Numbers 13. 1, 2, 25–end

The Promised Land is full of delights – milk, honey, and fruits – but the residents are formidable.

'We felt no bigger than grasshoppers, and that is how we must have been in their eyes' (v. 33).

Revelation 14. 14–end

This is the harvest of souls. The angel with 'authority over fire' is a terrifying figure. We need Dante to do it justice.

*

Saturday evening

Deuteronomy 30. 1–14 (15–end)

Lord, I love you with all my heart and soul.

'He will again rejoice and be good to you, as he rejoiced over your forefathers' (v. 10).

2 Peter 1. 1–11

The calling of God makes fundamental claims on our behaviour. With the honour of that calling, we should do no less than love with the love that he showed us.

O Lord, may your grace and peace be ours in fullest measure, through knowing you.

WEEKDAYS FOLLOWING THE FIFTH SUNDAY OF EASTER

Monday morning

Numbers 14. 1, 26–35

The Lord is exasperated with the murmurings and complaints of the Israelites and threatens to fulfil the prophecy the Israelites have themselves pronounced: that they will die in wilderness. Murmuring is a type of faithlessness.

Revelation 15. 1–4

This is deeply imbued with echoes from Moses and the Book of Exodus. The seven plagues represent the wrath of God. This is the new judgement, and those who are victorious against the beast sing out:

'Great and wonderful are your deeds
Lord God the Almighty' (ASB).

*

Monday evening

Deuteronomy 31. 1–8, 14–18

Moses speaks his last words and the Lord responds.

Be strong, be resolute: do not dread or be afraid, for the Lord your God himself goes with you; he will not fail you or forsake you.

2 Peter 1. 12–15

A personal note from Peter about a sense of imminent death or from a member of the Petrine school who feels able to sign the letter on Peter's behalf, helps us to give thanks for Peter's apostleship as the fisher of souls.

Tuesday morning

Numbers 20. 1–13

More complaints in the wilderness of Zin, to which Moses and Aaron react by going to the Tent of Meeting. The Lord commands Moses to strike water from the rock with his staff:

'Water gushed out in abundance and they all drank, men and animals' (v. 11).

Lord, let me not waver in faith, believing that you can bring the water of the Spirit out of the hard rock of my heart.

Revelation 19. 1–10

This reads like one great hymn interleaved with prose comment.

'Hallelujah! Victory and glory and power belong to our God' (v. 1).

Lord God, make me a fellow servant who bears witness to Jesus, and has the spirit of prophecy.

*

Tuesday evening

Deuteronomy 31.23 – 32.4

The Lord gives Joshua his commission to take the Israelites into the Promised Land, and gets Moses to write down a song, which will declare the Lord's anger at their wrongdoing. It begins beautifully:

'May my teaching fall like raindrops, my words distil like dew' (32.2).

2 Peter 1. 16–end

Shine, O Lord, like a lamp in my soul, murky as it is, until day breaks and the morning star rises to illuminate my mind.

Wednesday morning

Numbers 21. 4–9

Moses sets up a serpent, so that those bitten by a poisonous snake should recover. The lifting up of a model of iniquity becomes the salvation. So Christ becomes one of the transgressors, and is lifted up for our salvation.

Revelation 19. 11–16

The horse and the rider have a wide-ranging responsibility to speak faithfully and truly, from the word of God, to the nations.

Let us pray for those who have to speak to the nations.

*

Wednesday evening

Deuteronomy 32. 45–end

Take to heart the warnings, which we are spared.

2 Peter 2. 1–3

One sign of falseness in teaching is the place of money. Where there is greed for money, then there is likely to be fabrication.

Thursday morning

Numbers 22. 4b–6, 12–21, 36 – 23.3

Balak, King of Moab, summons Balaam from the east, the area of the Euphrates, to help him defeat the Israelites. Lancelot Andrewes picks up Matthew's point and likens the journey of Balaam to the journey of the Magi (Matt. 2.1).

Revelation 20. 1–4, 11–end

The roll – the list, the register – contains the names of those whose deeds have warranted them a place in the Kingdom of God.

'For a thousand years in your sight
 are like yesterday when it is past
and like a watch in the night' (Ps. 90.4).

*

Thursday evening

Deuteronomy 33. 1–12

Verses 2–5 are an introductory psalm. Verses 6–12 are a description of the tribes at a fairly late stage of their development in which changes have taken place. The Lord's love of Benjamin has placed Benjamin, in the Hebrew, 'between his shoulders' – like St Christopher with the child Jesus.

2 Peter 2. 4–10a

The author's dogmatic account of immorality and its consequences has a biblical heritage. Noah and Lot were saved by their good lives; others, even including angels, were not spared.

Lord, I am not worthy.

Friday morning

Numbers 23. 4–26

Despite elaborate plans by Balak to weight the decision of Balaam, Balaam can but prophesy as the Lord instructs him, and the Lord tells him to bless Israel.

Lord, give me that clearness of vision and strength of heart, which will help me to say only what you want me to say.

Revelation 21. 1–8

The nature of the Kingdom has its aesthetic quality – its newness, its white throne of victory – but it is also a Kingdom of justice and moral order. Its comprehensiveness lies in God himself, who is Alpha and Omega, beginning and end.

✳

Friday evening

Deuteronomy 33. 13–end

Verses 26–29 are the conclusion of the psalm begun at verse 1. The family history is very revealing. They are all very different, as we say, and it has the air of a Last Will and Testament.

2 Peter 2. 10b–16

Some of the sins that threaten the purity of the Church are: submission to raw instinct, violence, lust, and greed. Balaam (Num. 22–24) is brought in as an example. Even his donkey had to teach him.

✠

Saturday morning

Numbers 24. 1–19

Balaam has a beautiful description of Israel's camp:

'Jacob, how fair are your tents …
like gardens by a river …
like cedars beside the waters',

and his prophecy links forward to the Magi from the east:

'a star will come forth from Jacob,
a comet will arise from Israel.'

Revelation 21. 9–21

Temple and city become one. There is no need any longer for a special place to beseech God. The prayer is answered. St John furiously weaves all the biblical strands into his tapestry: bride, lamb, apostles, and the ark.

'The great street of the city was of pure gold' (v. 21).

*

Saturday evening

Deuteronomy 34

The priestly conclusion to Deuteronomy combines a pragmatic description of land to be enjoyed, and the strength of character that was Moses' as he walked with God for his people.

'Remember the strong hand of Moses and the awesome deeds which he did in the sight of all Israel' (v. 12).

2 Peter 2. 17–end

The converts have come out of a life of sin, and have entered a new state in Christ Jesus. What a shame when they are turned backwards! Living a Christian life with such high standards, in a secular world, is a very difficult thing.

Lord, I am not worthy.

✠

WEEKDAYS FOLLOWING THE SIXTH SUNDAY OF EASTER

Monday morning

Joshua 1. 1–11

Joshua succeeds Moses as leader of the Israelites and is responsible for seeing them into the Promised Land, across the Jordan. Courage, and a strong grasp of the Book of the Law, are essential.

'How sweet are your words to my taste!
they are sweeter than honey to my mouth'
(Ps. 119.103).

Revelation 21.22 – 22.5

Consciously returning to the beginning of Genesis, John portrays the water of life and the tree of life: images of faithfulness. Now it is possible to eat the fruit, because Christ has overturned the sin of Adam.

'… no darkness nor dazzling, but one equal radiance …' (John Donne)

✳

Monday evening

Joshua 3

As the Israelites went through the Red Sea on dry land, at the beginning of the Exodus, so the priests carrying the Ark of the Covenant go through the River Jordan, dryshod, at the end of the journey.

2 Peter 3. 1–10

The author of this letter had to help the Church reconcile itself to an extended period before the appearance of the Kingdom, and to explain the purpose of God's delay. Time has different qualities and lengths in God's mind.

✠

Tuesday morning

Joshua 5.13 – 6.10, 17–20

The famous walls of Jericho which came 'tumbling down', came down because it was the Lord's will. The Ark of the Covenant was with them.

Revelation 2. 6–15

'It is God you must worship' (v. 9). There is a similar harshness of moral censure as in 2 Peter.

*

Tuesday evening

Joshua 6. 22–25; 7. 1, 16–end

We may find the priorities strange here: slaughtering a whole community, and then pursuing an act of theft to the death. It probably means we have not got quite inside the Hebrew mind.

2 Peter 3. 11–end

There is an innocent bluntness in the conclusion of this letter. Paul is misunderstood, it says, and there is a sense of dependence on the Book of Revelation, for the mechanics of the final days.

Wednesday morning

Joshua 24. 1–2a, 14–29

Joshua's last words declare that, through his long experience, the Lord is a holy God, and a jealous God, who will not forgive rebellion. Joshua calls a people to choose. The people answer, 'We shall serve the Lord' (v. 21).

Revelation 22. 16–end

Come, offspring of David,
bright star of dawn.
Come, thirsty ones and drink the water of life.
Come, Lord Jesus.

*

Wednesday evening

Daniel 7. 9–14

In this great and terrifying court scene, in which the beasts are condemned, God sits in judgement. At that moment, the human figure appears and sits at God's right hand, and the whole picture of sovereignty takes on the proportion of justice and hope.

Just and true are your ways, O King of the Nations.

Revelation 5

The same Daniel figure, 'like a human being', becomes in Revelation the Christ who was crucified, the Lamb who was slain. Again, at the heart of the pomp is the vulnerable human figure, like us, with whom we can relate and associate.

Lord, you know me through and through, and you will be there in our time of need.

Ascension Day morning

Ezekiel 1. 4–5, 26–end

Ezekiel, the priest in exile, has the vision of a human figure, enthroned and encircled in the radiance of a rainbow after rain. It was the appearance of God in a human being.

Hebrews 1. 1–6

The Son 'took his seat at the right hand of God's majesty on high' (v. 3). The humanity of Jesus is exalted and seated in glory. He makes a wonderful central pivot, or balance, between earth longing for redemption, and heaven full of the redeemed.

Praise be to him for ever; glory in the heavens, world without end.

*

Ascension Day evening

2 Kings 2. 1–15

'... and Elijah was carried up to heaven in a whirlwind' (v. 11). Elisha witnessed it and that allowed him a double share of Elijah's spirit. The chariot in which Elijah ascended was made of fire: living, vibrant, powerful, cleansing.

'You clearly see the true Lord, possessor of the victory, passing into heaven' (*The Exeter Book*).

Hebrews 2. 9–end

Jesus went from earth to heaven, so that we might know there is hope for us there, and extravagant love on earth for us to follow him.

'Let us found our hopeful expectation upon that port which the Ruler of the skies, the Holy one in the heights, laid open to us when he ascended into the heavens' (*The Exeter Book*).

Pentecost

Friday morning

Exodus 35.30 – 36.1

The skill of hand and eye, and the generosity of Spirit, combine to decorate the place of worship; and all that helps to give worth is worthy too.

John 1. 29–34

Like the bird that ventures into flight, the one who ascends is the one on whom the Spirit descended: 'This is God's Chosen One.'

*

Friday evening

1 Samuel 10. 1–10

The beginning of the reign of Saul, anointed by Samuel, is one example of how kingship is taken on and begins, how it sets the scene for a future rule. The donkeys, and the meetings with men carrying things, reminds us of the beginning of Jesus' reign, from the Last Supper onwards.

Luke 4. 14–21

Inklings of the power of the Spirit meet in Christ and Isaiah. The meeting is dynamic, and sets Jesus' ministry going. This is what Jesus has the power to effect, and it is happening 'now'.

✠

Saturday morning

1 Kings 19. 1–16

Elijah, in despondency and under a broom bush, meets God in the still, small voice. He is given instructions to anoint kings, and to prepare for his own death by anointing Elisha to take his place. All because of a 'great zeal for the Lord'.

Matthew 9.35 – 10.8

The twelve disciples are given authority, first of all to do the healing work of Christ, which was also the bringing in of the Kingdom. They are the labourers for the heavy crop.

✳

Saturday evening

Jeremiah 31. 31–34

The day of Pentecost is coming. It comes – and comes as the new Spirit; the Holy Spirit is written into the hearts of God's chosen ones, and they are recreated.

Veni Creator Spiritus. Come, Creator Spirit.

Ephesians 4. 7–16

Growing and building, and being helped to grow and to be built, is a process. It takes time to find our gift, our very selves, and to be fully grown up into Christ.

Take my heart, it is thine own,
it shall be thy royal throne (Frances Ridley Havergal).

✠

WEEKDAYS FOLLOWING THE SEVENTH SUNDAY OF EASTER

Monday morning

Isaiah 32. 9–end

'... Until a spirit from on high is lavished upon us'. We wait on the Holy Spirit to transform our lives, the Church and society. This is figured here as a renewal in nature. The Spirit turns a wilderness into a garden.

Romans 5. 1–5

Lord, flood my heart with love
through the gift of the Holy Spirit,
that I may exult in the hope of
the divine glory.

*

Monday evening

Wisdom 1. 1–7

The spirit enters into the very marrow of the bone of a person, distinguishing falsehood from truth. The spirit is here equated with wisdom.

'... with each breath we breathe out, we call out the Spirit,
with each breath we breathe in, we hallow in the Spirit.'

(From Lancelot Andrewes.)

Galatians 5. 16–25

The Holy Spirit affects our whole nature, and who we are and what we do reflect our closeness to the Spirit. The famous list of the fruits ('harvest', NEB) of the Spirit are all qualities above and beyond the reach of law.

To us, O Lord,
your sevenfold gifts impart.

✠

Tuesday morning

Isaiah 44. 1–5

The spirit – the *ruah* in Hebrew, the breath of God – will bring the children blessing, 'like a green tamarisk, like willows by flowing streams' (v. 4).

'They are like trees planted by streams of water, bearing fruit in due season' (Ps. 1.3).

1 John 5. 6–12

Three things mark out the Christian: the water of baptism; the blood of compassion and the Eucharist; and the Spirit. The Spirit is truth. 'What is truth?' asked Pilate. The truth is God's way.

I believe in the Holy Spirit – as a power from on high from within and invisibly, but effectively and evidently transforming us into holiness.

(From Lancelot Andrewes.)

Tuesday evening

Wisdom 7.15 – 8.1

This intensely moving hymn to wisdom (*sophia*) likens it to 'a spirit intelligent and holy'.

Titus 2. 11–14; 3. 4–7

The Holy Spirit is a gift which comes through Jesus Christ.

'... from the Spirit to receive the breath of the grace that brings salvation' (Lancelot Andrewes).

✠

Wednesday morning

Ezekiel 11. 14–20

Lord, grant me singleness of heart and put a new spirit within me.

1 Corinthians 2. 1–13

Paul sees the Spirit as the essence of God, the very driving force of God, his power and his truth. It is that Spirit we have been given by God, in order to see things his way.

*

Wednesday evening

Wisdom 9. 13–end

The spirit is the means of knowing God. We cannot know God by any human means of our own devising, but only from the spirit, from heaven on high.

'Gracious Spirit, Holy Ghost,
taught by thee, we covet most
of thy gifts at Pentecost
holy, heavenly love.'

(Christopher Wordsworth)

1 Corinthians 3. 9–17

We are God's temple where the Spirit of God dwells. We house the Spirit, walk with it, talk with it, breathe with it. That is both a responsibility and a strength.

I believe that the Spirit is the Lord and Giver of life. You that gave me a living soul, grant that I may not have received my soul for nothing.
(Lancelot Andrewes)

✠

Thursday morning

Ezekiel 36. 22–28

It is not just for our own improvement that we should be given a new spirit and a new heart, although that is much needed; it is because God sees us as his standard-bearers.

2 Corinthians 3. 1–11

God has 'empowered us as ministers of a new covenant, not written but spiritual'. It is written on our hearts, and gives life.

'Let everything that has breath
praise the Lord.
  Alleluia!' (Ps. 150.6).

✳

Thursday evening

Micah 3. 1–8

Where there is no spirit, there is no vision, and there is moral chaos. It is difficult to see which comes first, but here Micah is saying that the prophets are leading the people astray. Justice and goodness must be at the heart of spirituality.

Lord, let us, like Micah, be full of strength to declare to this society its crime, its sin.

2 Corinthians 3. 12–end

It is by the Spirit of God that we can look God full in the face. The veil is taken away and we can be transformed by gazing into the face of Christ.

O Lord, transform us into your likeness.

✠

Friday morning

Ezekiel 37. 1–14

God is in charge. He performs miracles, through the communicating skills of Ezekiel, to make his name glorified. We come alive not for our own sake but to give God the glory.

Romans 8. 1–17

Paul describes, from his own experience, what the spiritual life is like. There could be no better explanation – although it takes some understanding, some accepting, and some living out.

'You live by the Spirit, since God's Spirit dwells in you' (v. 9).

Friday evening

Joel 2. 21–31

The pouring out of the spirit will precede the coming of the 'great and terrible day of the Lord'. The power of the spirit brings with it the terror of its responsibility.

'Your old men will dream dreams
and your young men see vision' (v. 28).

Romans 8. 18–27

In our stumbling inarticulacy and in the difficult times of growth, the Spirit, the Comforter, and Advocate, takes up his home in us, and shares the work of prayer.

Thanks be to God;
take my lips and speak through them.

✠

Saturday morning

Deuteronomy 16. 9–15

'You shall keep the feast with joy': and so we prepare for the Feast of Pentecost, seven weeks after Easter Day. Rejoice ... rejoice ... !

'And in the Temple of the Lord,
all are crying, "Glory!"' (Ps. 29.9)

Luke 11. 1–13

Prayer is asking the Father, 'Abba, Father', which is the beginning of the Lord's Prayer. We must ask.

Abba, Heavenly Father,
inspire us, we pray.

*

Saturday evening

Genesis 11. 1–9

Quite often a perceived reality – such as the conflict of cultures, symbolized by language – is, because of the overall rule of God, traced back to the will of God. Why it was God's will to scatter is understood as we understand 'I have come not to bring peace, but a sword' (Matt. 10.34).

Isaiah 61. 1–9

The spirit of the Lord leads us into the love and care of our neighbour. It is not just a facility to make us feel holy, but a social power: 'Buildings long in ruins will be rebuilt.'

Lord, lover of justice, preserve us from the narrow vision.

Year A *John 7. 37–39*

On the last and greatest day of the Feast of Tabernacles, Jesus announces that those who believe in him shall, in time, receive the Holy Spirit.

'Streams of living water shall flow from within [them]' (v. 38).

or John 14. 15–26

Jesus, conscious of the imminent end of his bodily life, comforts the disciples with the news that they will have the Spirit of truth for ever. That Spirit, we believe, is God, indissolubly part of the Holy Trinity.

Year B *John 7. 37–39 or Acts 18.24 – 19.7*

From very early in the life of the Christian Church it was at baptism that it was felt that the Holy Spirit descended, in the same way as at John's baptism of Jesus.

Year C *John 7. 37–39 or Ephesians 6. 10–20*

O Heavenly Father
hold me up with your Holy Spirit,
as the sea the boat,
as the air the bird,
as the mother the child,
and as Christ was upheld by the cross
to win the victory for a fallen world.

After Pentecost

WEEKDAYS AFTER THE DAY OF PENTECOST

Monday morning

Judges 2. 11–19

Earthly judges come and go. In their time they help the people resist the worship of the Baalim. The Baalim have eyes but see not, ears but hear not. The people await a God who can see and hear and love.

Come, Lord Jesus.

Acts 2. 14, 22–36

The God who could defeat death has risen and reigns, and is worshipped, followed, and adored by those who have received the gift of the Holy Spirit.

'My heart is glad
and my tongue rejoices;
moreover, my flesh shall dwell in hope'
(v. 26).

*

Monday evening

Ezra 1. 1–6

'Build me a home at Jerusalem.' 'Rebuild my Church,' said God to St Francis of Assisi. So Francis got the stones, one on top of another, and cleared out the mess, and rejoiced in his work.

Philippians 1. 1–11

'My prayers are always joyful.' When Paul thinks of Christ's people in Philippi, he rejoices because he knows that Christ is with them, and they are waiting on the coming of Christ.

Tuesday morning

Judges 4. 4–7, 12–22

Two worlds confront us: the world of military death, intrigue, campaigns, all in some primitive way working towards God's renewed world; and the other world of the resurrection. We wait.

Lord, have mercy.

Acts 2. 37–end

The resurrection community of repentance, in receipt of the Holy Spirit, is another world: the day after the night, the sun after the storm.

'I will give thanks to you, O Lord, with my
whole heart;
I will tell of all your marvellous works'
(Ps. 9.1).

*

Tuesday evening

Ezra 3

'Rejoice with those who rejoice' (Rom. 12.15). So we rejoice with those who have rebuilt the Temple, to offer praise and sacrifice to God.

Philippians 1. 12–26

Paul is rejoicing, though he is in prison. He rejoices that Christ is being proclaimed.

'So our eyes look to the Lord our God' (Ps. 123.3).

✠

Wednesday morning

Judges 6. 11–24

Gideon, aware that these are less exciting days, and living in a real and violent world, tries to do the will of God as best he can.

'As for all the gods of the nations, they are but idols; but it is the Lord who made the heavens' (Ps. 96.5).

Acts 3. 1–10

Peter and John's confrontation with the world of disease and poverty is with the name of the Lord Jesus on their lips.

Wednesday evening

Ezra 4. 1–8a, 17–23

The restoration is beset by problems: progress in God's work is never smooth. It needs great courage and persuasion.

Philippians 1. 27–end

The days of serving the Lord Jesus in the early period of the Church's life was not easy.

'For you have been granted the privilege not only of believing in Christ, but also of suffering for him' (v. 29).

Thursday morning

Judges 7. 1–8, 15–22

Gideon is closely associated with the Lord in all that he plans. Details matter. All of life is put at the disposal of the Lord.

Acts 3. 11–end

Peter announces that victory will only come through repentance and turning to God. Listen to God's instructions, turn to God and hear them.

Thursday evening

Haggai 1. 1–11

The imperative to build the Temple came even before the building of the private houses in Jerusalem. The failure to build a Temple is the cause of natural disasters.

Philippians 2. 1–11

This is the story of God's humility, in the life and death of Christ Jesus. Because of his faithful humility, he is to be worshipped and adored above all others.

Friday morning

Judges 9. 6–15, 21, 50–end

Abimelech, who slew his seventy brothers in his ambition to be king, meets his just end, as a millstone is dropped on his head. Evil is punished. God holds sway.

Acts 4. 1–12

Peter and John proclaim the resurrection and the power of the name of Jesus, to 'the powers that be' in Jerusalem.

*

Friday evening

Haggai 1.15b – 2.9

The destruction of the Temple is a great shame to God, and with its renewal will come the restoration of the people, based on the Temple.

Philippians 2. 12–18

Paul asks the Philippian Christians to be examples of the Christ-like life, and he declares his own commitment to them, in their suffering and their joy.

Saturday morning

Judges 11. 29–end

Alas for the daughter of Jephthah the Gileadite! O all you prayerful people, virgins among you, pray for her and give thanks that Christ has released us from such vows.

Acts 4. 13–31

May the power and the glory and the joy of the early Christian proclamations be ours too.

*

Saturday evening

Exodus 3. 1–6

Moses sees the bush burning but it is not consumed. He sees the glory of the Lord, who is an historical God of his fathers and fathers' fathers: of Abraham, Isaac and Jacob.

Revelation 4

Holy, holy, holy is God,
the sovereign Lord of all,
who was, and is, and is to come.
Alleluia. Amen.

✠

WEEKDAYS FOLLOWING THE FIRST SUNDAY AFTER PENTECOST (TRINITY SUNDAY)

Monday morning

Judges 13. 1–7

Samson's birth is announced to his mother, who is not named. He is destined to be a great champion of the Israelite faith, and his life is to follow the strict rules of the Nazirites.

'He makes the woman of a childless house
to be a joyful mother of children' (Ps. 113.8).

Acts 4.32 – 5.11

The Early Church held their possessions in common and while Barnabas is shown as a good example of this practice, Ananias and his wife Sapphira hold back part of their wealth, lying against the Holy Spirit, and die. The importance of generous sharing is the underlying theme of this passage.

*

Monday evening

Zechariah 1.18 – 2.5

Here are three visions and a promise: the horns which scattered Judah; four smiths to rout those who were scattering; a man with a measuring line, which indicated the future prosperity of Jerusalem. The promise is of the Lord's presence which will be like a wall of fire.

Lord, be to us a wall of fire and a glorious presence.

Philippians 2.19 – 3.1

At its heart the Church has the presence of Christ, but then there are the members, and here are three of its greatest servants: Paul himself; Timothy, like a son of his; and Epaphroditus, Paul's fellow-worker, each a limb of the Body of Christ.

✠

Tuesday morning

Judges 16. 4–22

The secret of Samson's strength is betrayed by Delilah to his enemies, the Philistines. The betrayal is a foretaste of the betrayal of Jesus by Judas.

'My strength is dried up like a potsherd' (Ps. 22.15, AV).

Acts 5. 12–26

Even Peter's shadow has a healing power. The Church, and particularly the Apostles, having received great spiritual strength at Pentecost, are now delivered by an angel from prison. These are exciting days.

'I sat down under his shadow with great delight' (S. of S. 2.3, AV).

*

Tuesday evening

Zechariah 3

Joshua, the high priest, stands under judgement, in filthy clothes, before God. He is acquitted. More than that, he is to lead his people into a bright future. He is also to be the Branch, mentioned in the great prophetic verse, verse 8.

Philippians 3. 2–16

Set against mere outward observance of ritual such as circumcision, Paul places an inward and spiritual relationship with Christ, which is all-consuming. The motive for this is that at the end of suffering with Christ, we shall receive the prize of rising with him.

Wednesday morning

Judges 16. 23–end

Samson dies, and the end of his captors comes at the same time, with the destruction of the building where he was bound. The wheat and the tares grow together until the day of God's judgement.

'All is best, though we oft doubt
What the unsearchable dispose
Of Highest Wisdom brings about,
And ever best found in the close.'
(John Milton, *Samson Agonistes*)

Acts 5. 27–end

Gamaliel gives his wise advice on the followers of Christ, and their way:

'If what is being planned and done in human in origin, it will collapse; but if it is from God, you will never be able to stamp it out' (v. 39).

*

Wednesday evening

Corpus Christi

Exodus 16. 2–15

The Lord will provide. Even in the desert he feeds his people with manna
from heaven. The miracle of feeding
takes us forward to the feeding of the five thousand in the New Testament.

John 6. 22–35

St John specifically echoes the story of the desert banquet, with Jesus' feeding of the five thousand. The point which John pursues here is the great miracle of nourishment, as the chimes of the gospel bell ring out and Jesus says,

'I am the bread of life' (v. 35).

Acts 20. 5–12

Paul and the Christians at Troas meet for the breaking of the bread, and poor, sleepy Eutychus falls out of the window. Paul declares he is alive. They 'broke bread and ate' (v. 11).

✠

Thursday morning

Corpus Christi

Year A *Exodus 24. 1–11*

Moses is the one whom God appoints to arrange the sacrifices which will unite God and his people. This unity is also called a covenant, in which, as a ceremonial act, the reading of the Law takes a crucial part. Early on, we see word and sacrament together.

'Let us obey, and do everything that the Lord has told us' (v. 3).

Mark 14. 12–25

In Mark's account of the Last Supper, Jesus unites the bread with his body, the wine with the shedding of his blood for many, and both with his imminent entry into God's Kingdom.

'You spread a table before me
in the presence of those who trouble me'
(Ps. 23.5).

Year B *Genesis 14. 18–20*

Blessing and eating takes place between Melchisedek and Abram. They praise God and thank him for their deliverance. We see the seeds of the Eucharist.

Luke 9. 11–17

Jesus takes the initiative in the feeding of the five thousand.

'The eyes of all wait upon you, O Lord,
and you give them their food in due season'
(Ps. 145.16).

Year C *Deuteronomy 8. 2–16*

Moses gives a great discourse on the blessings of the Lord God.

'People cannot live on bread alone, but … they live on every word that comes from the mouth of the Lord' (v. 3).

John 6. 51–58

Christ says that the bread that lasts for ever is his own flesh, which we must 'eat'. It is not easy to know with St John how spiritual and how material he is being. The two come very close to each other in Christ.

*

Thursday evening

Corpus Christi

Year A *Genesis 14. 18–20*

Luke 9. 11–17

Year B *Deuteronomy 8. 2–16*

John 6. 51–58

Year C *Exodus 24. 1–11*

Mark 14. 12–25

For the readings on Thursday Evening (Corpus Christi) see the commentary on the readings for the morning.

✠

Friday morning

1 Samuel 1. 1–8

The birth of Samuel is preceded by the story of his mother Hannah's humiliation. The drama centres on the temple at Shiloh. Even Elkanah, her husband, does not understand her grief. Hannah shows great devotion, as Mary does after her in the New Testament.

Acts 6

Seven deacons are appointed. Stephen is one of them. Stephen is a beautiful Christian character, full of grace and power.

'[Moses'] face shone because he had been talking with the Lord' (Exod. 34.29).

*

Friday evening

Zechariah 4

With strong echoes bouncing back from the Book of Revelation, Zechariah is again seeing things which help him understand the present moment. His enemy Zerubbabel is not to be feared. Small things are to be treasured. The rock of might is not to be compared to the oil of holiness.

'Who has despised the day of small things?' (v. 10)

Philippians 3.17 – 4.1

The human body, which can be such an ass, can also be transformed into a glorious body, as we stand beside Christ and share his glory. We too can be transfigured.

Lord, transfigure our humble bodies.

Saturday morning

1 Samuel 1. 9–20

Eli, the priest at Shiloh, also mistakes Hannah's grief, but then he blesses her and the divine seed grows into its fulfilment in Samuel. The name means, 'I asked the Lord for him'.

Acts 7. 1–16

Stephen's address to the High Priest is a recital of the great history of faith. Although the Holy Spirit came at Pentecost, the roots of faith go much deeper down, beginning with Abraham.

*

Saturday evening

Zechariah 6. 9–end

Joshua is to be crowned and he will also be the Branch who will reach out and be the instrument of the rebuilding of the Temple. The vine and the branches and the crown will emerge again in the rebuilding of the new temple, not made with hands, in the person of Christ.

'Jesus said … "You see these great buildings?" ' (Mark 13.2)

Philippians 4. 2–20

These are the final words of a moving letter about the hallmarks of a Christian character, which are joy, harmony, and mutual care one for another. Each member of the growing Church needs the other, and all need to be made complete in Christ.

WEEKDAYS FOLLOWING THE SECOND SUNDAY AFTER PENTECOST

Monday morning

1 Samuel 3. 1–10, 19–20

God calls the boy Samuel in the night, and Samuel turns to an incredulous Eli to share the mystery of the call. Good advice is eventually given to Samuel. To the call of God he is recommended to say,

'Speak, Lord; your servant is listening.'

Acts 7. 17–34

Stephen continues his address to the Jews, with a description of the place of Moses in the history of salvation. We continue to be made aware of the shared depth of the tradition in which we live.

'He made his ways known to Moses
and his works to the children of Israel'
(Ps. 103.7).

*

Monday evening

Haggai 2. 10–end

Here we have the third prophecy which predicts a return of fertility to the land (vv. 11–19), and the fourth (vv. 20–24) which promises Zerubbabel's victory over his enemies. Zerubbabel is the governor of Judah.

2 Corinthians 1. 1–11

Consolation, with mutual sharing of one another's burdens, is an essential part of the Christian life. It goes alongside a trusting dependence on God's power to deliver us from the worst of problems or 'perils'.

✠

Tuesday morning

1 Samuel 4. 1–11

Oppressed by the Philistines, the Israelites wonder why the Lord has deserted them. Their attempts to restore their self-esteem also fail. The Ark of the Covenant is stolen, and Eli's sons are killed.

Acts 7. 35–53

Stephen continues his address with a description of the work of Moses, and then of Joshua, David, and Solomon. It is with the Temple that the address turns into polemic. The temple not made with hands, Christ, has been killed, and the law has not been kept.

✳

Tuesday evening

Ezra 6. 6–20

The intensity, excitement, and commitment aroused by the Temple of the Lord show how vivid it was as a symbol of home. It was crucial that it should be restored, and that they should rejoice and sacrifice in it once more.

2 Corinthians 1. 12–22

'Yes to God' is a splendid acclamation, but we say it, says St Paul, in Christ. We don't say it on our own, but through Christ, to God, who then sends his Spirit to dwell in our hearts.

✠

Wednesday morning

1 Samuel 6.13 – 7.1

The stolen Ark of the Lord is on the move in the possession of the Philistines, but it is wreaking havoc among the unfaithful. The people of Beth-shemesh don't want it, and are pleased to give it to the men of Kiriath-jearim; both places are about twenty miles west of Jerusalem.

'Moses and Aaron among his priests,
and Samuel among those who call upon his
name ...' (Ps. 99.6)

Acts 7.54 – 8.3

The stoning of Stephen with his eyes gazing heaven-wards, and the still and silent presence of the young Saul, looking after the coats of those doing the stoning, make one of those pictures of the human spirit meeting the divine which remain fixed for ever.

Wednesday evening

Zechariah 8. 1–8, 20–end

This is a vision of peace and security in which people and God are at one, and Jerusalem is the home for all the nations. It is a picture of harmony, an ideal to hold before ourselves, and to work for.

'They will be my people, and I shall be their God, in faithfulness and justice'
(v. 8).

2 Corinthians 1.23 – 2.4

The real personal anxiety that St Paul describes here shows his humanity. The cause of the anxiety comes from a challenge to his authority. In his response, love and pain are deeply entwined.

✠

Thursday morning

1 Samuel 8. 4–7, 10–22a

To appoint a king is seen, in some sense, to depose God as king, and so both Samuel and the Lord are against it. The people, however, are keen to appoint one, and the whole process is shrouded in problems, arising out of the desire to be like other nations.

Acts 8. 4–8

Philip is listened to with respect in Samaria as he proclaims the Messiah and heals those who are sick in body and mind.

*

Thursday evening

Ezra 7. 1–10, 27–end

The arrival of Ezra, priest and scribe, from Babylon back into Jerusalem, is described with loving attention to his scholarship, holiness, and his favour in the eyes of King Artaxerxes.

'The favour of God was with him, for he had devoted himself to the study and observance of the law of the Lord' (vv. 9–10).

2 Corinthians 2. 5–end

The authority of Paul that was questioned was his authority to forgive, and a difficult matter of discipline seems to have been solved. Two telling images help the truth to be felt: we are captives in Christ's triumphal procession, and we convey Christ's fragrance.

✠

Friday morning

The Divine Compassion

Jeremiah 30. 18–22

This vision of the compassion of God towards his people is put in very practical ways: their dwellings will be restored, but, also in the deepest sense of belonging,

'You will be my people,
and I shall be your God' (v. 22).

Ephesians 1. 1–14

This is a very wide vision of the unity of all things in Christ. We are drawn into that unity through God's will, accepted in faith, and sealed by the Holy Spirit.

*

Friday evening

Jeremiah 31. 31–34

The law, observed with external ritual, is now to be written on the hearts of people, as a sign of God's favour towards them.

Romans 8. 28–end

The bond between God and the individual believer – in this case Paul, although he is a representative of all who love God – is so strong that nothing can break it.

Nothing ... can separate us from the love of God in Christ Jesus our Lord.

Saturday morning

1 Samuel 10. 17–end

The appointment of Saul to be king is surrounded by ambivalent emotions. The Lord sees it as disobedience. Samuel organizes it, but his companions are against it. Saul, discovered among the bags, seems destined for failure. God's will has not been listened to.

Acts 8. 26–end

A vivid portrait of the journey of faith takes place on a real journey from Jerusalem to Gaza. Philip helps the eunuch from Ethiopia understand the scriptures of Isaiah and then baptizes him.

'Do you understand what you are reading?' 'How can I without someone to guide me?' (vv. 30, 31)

✳

Saturday evening

Ezra 9. 1–9

Attempts to re-establish a life of faith on returning from exile tax Ezra, particularly in regard to mixed marriages. Ezra makes a personal and classic act of repentance for the people's guilt.

I am humiliated, my God,
I am ashamed, my God,
to lift my face to you.

2 Corinthians 3. 12–end

The veil is the image which helps Paul describe the difference between the law and the grace which comes through Jesus Christ. The law is veiled. The veil is drawn back from the grace of Christ, revealed in glory, and the means of our transformation.

✠

WEEKDAYS FOLLOWING THE THIRD SUNDAY AFTER PENTECOST

Monday morning

1 Samuel 11. 5–end

Saul's victory over the Ammonites re-establishes his kingship, but his anger is an indication of the stormy times to come.

Acts 9. 1–9

Saul is stopped in his tracks near Damascus by Jesus who challenges him with the question, 'Why are you persecuting me?' No more dramatic conversion has ever been told, but in this particular passage only Paul's shock is recorded.

*

Monday evening

Nehemiah 1

Nehemiah's prayer sets all that happens in the light of God's providence. If we are faithful then things will go well; if disobedient, then the scattering of the people is inevitable.

2 Corinthians 4. 1–6

The openness of preaching is contrasted with the darkness of those who have something to hide. Paul proclaims Christ Jesus as Lord and ourselves as servants.

'He will bring to light what darkness hides and disclose our inward motives' (1 Cor. 4.5).

✠

Tuesday morning

1 Samuel 12, or 12. 1–2, 13–15, 22–end

It is all a matter of obedience. God's will is to be done. Everything rests on that, says the now white-haired Samuel.

'Do not be afraid; although you have been so wicked, do not give up the worship of the Lord, but serve him with all your heart' (v. 20).

Acts 9. 10–19a

Ananias is the chosen instrument of helping Paul move more deeply into his relationship with Jesus through the Church. He helps Paul open his eyes, baptizes him, and feeds him.

'Recover your sight and be filled with the Holy Spirit' (v. 17).

*

Tuesday evening

Nehemiah 2. 1–8

Nehemiah asks King Artaxerxes for permission to return to Judah to rebuild the Temple. His request is granted, and he puts this success down to the gracious hand of God.

2 Corinthians 4. 7–end

Amid all the difficulties that any human endeavour incurs comes this unique experience of dying with Christ, that in this body the life of Christ may be revealed.

Wednesday morning

1 Samuel 13. 3–15

Saul fails again in obedience to God by not waiting for Samuel to offer the sacrifices at Gilgal. Their ways divide and Saul takes his six hundred followers with him.

Acts 9. 19b–25

The time from Saul's conversion to beginning his teaching and proclaiming Jesus as Lord, openly, is rapid. Saul's enormous energy is now directed into the real purpose of his life, to serve Jesus the Messiah.

Wednesday evening

Nehemiah 4. 1–15

The building of the walls of Jerusalem is met with derision by Sanballat and Tobiah the Ammonite.

2 Corinthians 5. 1–10

Our physical body and our spiritual body are like a building within a building. The one cannot exist without the other but the physical can be absorbed into the spiritual, by the work of the Spirit.

✠

Thursday morning

1 Samuel 15. 10–23

The friction between Samuel and Saul flares up after Saul's defeat of the Amalekites, and over Saul's inadequate response to the commands of the Lord concerning sacrifices.

Acts 9. 26–30

The disciples in Jerusalem are frightened of Paul, but Barnabas explains the situation and recommends Paul to them. For his own security, Paul is sent away to Tarsus.

Be with us in our desert times of preparation.

Thursday evening

Nehemiah 5. 1–13

In the middle of famine, the social injustice of pledging members of the family for food is condemned by Nehemiah. He commands them to set right the wrongs and to live in the fear of God.

2 Corinthians 5. 11–17

The new creation inaugurated by Christ's disciples puts into a completely different perspective our attitude to others and to ourselves.

✠

Friday morning

1 Samuel 16. 1–13

From all the sons of Jesse, the Lord prompts Samuel to choose and anoint the youngest, David, as king.

'There is still the youngest … but he is looking after the sheep' (v. 11).

Acts 9. 31–35

Under the inspiration of the Holy Spirit the Church is growing, and in the name of Jesus Christ Peter heals Aeneas, bedridden for eight years.

*

Friday evening

Nehemiah 6. 1–15

Nehemiah, passionately keen to complete the wall, defies the attempts of his enemies to distract him.

2 Corinthians 5.18 – 6.2

Reconciliation, the harmony between people of different views, is also, Paul says, to be worked for between people and God.

Saturday morning

1 Samuel 17. 1–11, 37–50

The battle lines between the Philistines, and Saul and the Israelites, are drawn. Goliath boasts of his strength and the Israelites cower. David, in the strength of the Lord, slays the mighty Goliath.

'When I am weak, then I am strong'
(2 Cor. 12.10).

Acts 9. 36–end

Dorcas, maker of fine shirts, and one who spread around her light and love, is raised from the dead by Peter. The circumstances of this miracle are similar to Jesus' raising of Jairus' daughter.

*

Saturday evening

Nehemiah 8. 1–12

There is a reverence with which Ezra reads the book of the law, and a loving attention by those who are on the platform with him. The seriousness of the reading and the joy of the celebrations following it represent a fine balance of response to God's word.

'Your decrees are wonderful;
therefore I obey them with all my heart'
(Ps. 119.129).

2 Corinthians 6. 3–13

The way God's ministers should respond to suffering and hardship recommends itself both by joy and by its stark contrast to expected worldly standards.

✠

WEEKDAYS FOLLOWING THE FOURTH SUNDAY AFTER PENTECOST

Monday morning

1 Samuel 18. 1–16

David is a rising star, which aggravates Saul's instability and jealousy. The love that David and Jonathan have for one another has become proverbial.

'The soul of Jonathan was knit with the soul of David' (v. 1, AV).

Acts 10. 1–16

The fierce debate over what foods were permissible to the Jews is fuelled by Peter's vision in which he understands God's declaring all foods clean.

*

Monday evening

Nehemiah 8. 13–end

The eight days of the Festival of Booths, during which the law is read, is re-established with much dignity and rejoicing.

2 Corinthians 6.14 – 7.4

Paul speaks with his most severe voice about the need to remain holy, and at the same time at his most gentle in his declaration of affection for the Corinthian church.

'Proclaim the greatness of the Lord our God …
he is the Holy One' (Ps. 99.5).

Tuesday morning

1 Samuel 19. 1–12

Jonathan pleads for David before Saul, his father. Saul is still subject to fits of fierce anger, and David is encouraged to hide by his wife Michal.

Acts 10. 17–33

The extended combination of visions and journeys between the messenger of Cornelius and Simon Peter continues. Peter goes to Caesarea and reveals the Lord's words, 'Call nothing unclean.'

Tuesday evening

Nehemiah 9. 1–8, 32–37

The religious duties of the Israelites are described, and Nehemiah gives instructions as to what to say in prayer to the Lord.

2 Corinthians 7. 5–end

Titus arrives with comforting news to Paul, that his 'hard' letter is having an effect.

Wednesday morning

1 Samuel 20. 11–13, 18–20, 35–end

The love between David and Jonathan is given practical expression as Jonathan helps David escape from Saul.

Acts 10. 34–43

Peter delivers a Christian manifesto. It begins with the radical words, 'God has no favourites', continues with the story of Jesus, and ends with its working out in the Church. It is an eye-witness credo.

*

Wednesday evening

Nehemiah 13. 15–22, 28–end

The Sabbath is being destroyed by trade. Nehemiah sets a watch in place on the gates of the city, and checks that the Levites are doing their duty.

2 Corinthians 8. 1–7

The Macedonian church is praised for its generosity. The Corinthian church is commanded to be similarly generous, remembering always the Lord Jesus Christ, who became poor that we might become rich in spirit.

Thursday morning

1 Samuel 21.1 – 22.5

David's men eat the sacred bread. David continues to flee from Saul, which takes him through the territory of King Achish to the cave of Medullam, and he then places his parents into the care of the King of Moab.

'Have you never read what David did when he and his men were hungry?' (Mark 2.25)

Acts 10. 44–end

Through the agency of the Holy Spirit the width of God's love, to the Gentiles as well as the Jews, is recognized and celebrated by Peter, who baptizes many in the name of Jesus Christ.

*

Thursday evening

Jonah 1.1 – 2. 2, 10

Details of the escape of Jonah from the Lord's command includes the deeply symbolic period of three days and nights in the darkness of the whale's belly.

'The only sign that will be given ... is the sign of Jonah' (Luke 11.29).

2 Corinthians 8. 8–15

Sharing the resources of the Christian communities which Paul had set up was a priority.

Friday morning

1 Samuel 24

The conflict between David and Saul takes a surprising turn: David, in a position to kill Saul, spares his life; and Saul, when he is aware of this, laments his own failure in compassion.

'God forbid that I should harm my master, the Lord's anointed' (v. 4).

Acts 11. 1–18

By describing his vision once more, Peter tries to win over the Jewish church in Jerusalem to the plight of the Gentiles.

✳

Friday evening

Jonah 3

Jonah goes to Nineveh, preaches the word of God, and by both citizen and king the word is heard.

2 Corinthians 8. 16–end

Titus is praised for his leadership in handling the resources of the church.

Saturday morning

1 Samuel 28. 3–end

With the help of the witch of Endor, Saul summons up the ghost of Samuel. Samuel announces a chapter of disasters for Saul, because of his disobedience to the will of God.

Acts 11. 19–end

The growth of the Church among Gentiles as well as Jews is a matter of great importance to Luke in his authorship of Acts. Barnabas assists the work. He is a good man and full of the Holy Spirit.

✳

Saturday evening

Jonah 4

God is sorry for the people of Nineveh, and Jonah cannot countenance God's being so favourable towards them. The gourd withers under which Jonah is sitting and he is sorry. God uses this as an image of his desire to be sorry or compassionate for the foreign people of Nineveh.

'Should I not be sorry about the great city of Nineveh?' (v. 11)

2 Corinthians 9. 1–5

The collection around the churches of Paul's missionary endeavours proceeds apace.

✠

WEEKDAYS FOLLOWING THE FIFTH SUNDAY AFTER PENTECOST

Monday morning

1 Samuel 31

After his suicide and the desecration of his corpse by the Philistines, Saul's unhappy life and barbaric death find their rest under the tamarisk tree in Jabeth.

Acts 12. 1–11

Peter is rescued from the clutches of Herod by an angel, and he recognizes it as the work of the Lord.

Lord, help me to see you in the angels of this life.

*

Monday evening

Ruth 1. 1–18

The devotion Ruth shows to her mother-in-law issues in the most beautiful of statements:

'Where you go, I shall go, and where you stay, I shall stay. Your people will be my people, and your God my God' (v. 16).

2 Corinthians 9. 6–end

Paul writes in overwhelming praise of the generosity of the Corinthian church. He also reminds them that God loves a cheerful giver.

Tuesday morning

2 Samuel 1. 1–4, 11–12, 17–19, 23–end

David laments over Saul and Jonathan. Of Jonathan he says:

'You were most dear to me;
your love for me was wonderful,
surpassing the love of women.'

Acts 12. 12–24

Peter escapes to the house of John Mark's mother, Mary, and after initial amazement the church gathered in the house rejoice. The death of Herod is described in terms of his usurping the honour due to God.

*

Tuesday evening

Ruth 1.19 – 2.13

Ruth helps with the barley harvest and meets Boaz. Boaz is moved by Ruth's devotion to Naomi and calls on the Lord to reward her.

'A glad heart makes a cheerful face' (Prov. 15.13).

2 Corinthians 10. 1–12

Paul is certainly feeling threatened by the Corinthian church, and in a period of intense anxiety stumbles after a way of combining humility and weakness, with the strength that God supplies: 'I … appeal to you by the gentleness and magnaminity of Christ.'

✠

Wednesday morning

2 Samuel 5. 1–10

David takes Jerusalem from the Jebusites and the city is renamed the City of David. The Lord the God of Hosts is with David. Attitudes to the blind and the lame have changed since those days.

Acts 12.25 – 13.12

Paul and Barnabas reach Paphos and here Paul sees into the troubled spirit of Barjesus the sorcerer. Temporary blindness comes over Barjesus, and it is seen as an act of God, mediated through his apostle.

'Paul, filled with the Holy Spirit, fixed his eyes on him …' (v. 9) The fixed look of Paul is material for a great artist.

✳

Wednesday evening

Ruth 2. 14–end

Boaz shows great kindness and consideration to Ruth, and Naomi praises God for his providential care.

'Blessings on the man who took notice of you!' (v. 19)

2 Corinthians 10. 13–end

The spheres of mission are clearly demarcated and provide the basis for Paul's sense of responsibility, and his pride – not in himself, but in the Lord: 'If anyone would boast, let him boast of the Lord.'

Lord, let all my pride be in you, and therefore no pride will be allowed.

✠

Thursday morning

2 Samuel 6. 1–15

The extravagant side of David's character is revealed. He dances before the Ark of the Lord, but there are deep emotions running around, including his wife's hatred of him.

'Let them praise his name in the dance' (Ps. 149.3).

Acts 13. 13–25

In Pisidian Antioch Paul addresses the synagogue on the history of God's involvement with his people from the time of Abraham to John the Baptist.

*

Thursday evening

Ruth 3. 1–13

Ruth and Boaz are drawn closer together, and a happy ending to the story which began in such sadness is a blessing from the Lord.

2 Corinthians 11. 1–11

The twists and turns of Paul's response to the Corinthian church are mixed up with his eagerness to place Christ in the centre of his mission, and to get the financial situation clear.

Friday morning

2 Samuel 7. 4–17

David's destiny in the eyes of the Lord is great, but it is to David's son that the honour of building the Temple is to come.

Acts 13. 26–43

A central point in Paul's preaching is that Jesus is incorruptible.

'For you will not abandon me to the grave' (Ps. 16.10).

*

Friday evening

Ruth 3.14 – 4.6

Boaz makes arrangements with Naomi's next-of-kin concerning land which leaves the way open for him to marry Ruth.

2 Corinthians 11. 12–21a

Paul, with his back to the wall and confronted by a critical church, pours out an account of his religious credentials.

'Every day we gloried in God,
and we will praise your name for ever'
(Ps. 44.8).

✠

Saturday morning

2 Samuel 7. 18–end

David went into the presence of the Lord and asked for his blessing on his people, on his own leadership and on his 'house'.

O Lord God, you yourself know your servant. What you do, you do so that I may know more about you.

Acts 13. 44–end

The animosity between Jews and Gentiles reaches fever pitch in Antioch. The Gentiles respond to Paul's preaching, and the word of the Lord spreads through the region.

*

Saturday evening

Ruth 4. 7–end

The marriage and property transactions take place. Boaz marries Ruth and they have a child who they call Obed. The women say to Naomi:

'Blessed be the Lord, who has not left you this day without next-of-kin' (v. 14).

2 Corinthians 11. 21b–end

Credentials are one thing, sufferings another. This is a show of raw emotion by Paul, at which we are left wondering what our apostleship involves.

'He who is blessed for ever, the God and Father of the Lord Jesus, knows that what I say is true' (v. 31).

✠

WEEKDAYS FOLLOWING THE SIXTH SUNDAY AFTER PENTECOST

Monday morning

2 Samuel 9

Mephibosheth, crippled in both feet, takes his place at David's table, because he is a remaining member of Saul's family. This is the fulfilment of a promise, and an act of kindness, by David, for Jonathan's sake.

'Then the lame will leap like deer' (Isa. 35.6).

Acts 14. 1–7

Paul and Barnabas find themselves in the middle of a three-way conflict. It is between Jews sympathetic to Christians, Gentiles, and also Jews unsympathetic to Christians; but Paul and Barnabas speak out boldly in reliance on the Lord.

*

Monday evening

Esther 2. 5–11, 15–18

The preferential treatment which Ahasuerus gives to Esther, and the glowing description of Esther's beauty and charm, lead us to expect some form of danger.

2 Corinthians 12. 1–10

The infamous 'thorn in the flesh' is what holds Paul back from too much boasting. The weakness that this thorn symbolizes is, ironically, the root of his real strength, or dependence on God.

✠

Tuesday morning

2 Samuel 11. 1–17

David's desire for Bathsheba leads him into a devious scheme to get Uriah, Bathsheba's husband, killed in battle.

Acts 14. 8–18

Paul heals a man who has been lame from birth, and is met with great adulation which he tries to temper. His speech to them, about God in every person, echoes his thoughts in Romans 1.20.

Lord, let us not neglect the clues we have to your nature, in the benefits you bestow on us.

✳

Tuesday evening

Esther 3. 1–13

With chilling echoes of the holocaust we see the rise of Haman to power, and his desire to exterminate the alien Jews.

2 Corinthians 12. 11–18

The three visits of Paul to Corinth have had different outcomes. Here, the collection is played down: 'It is you I want, not your money.'

✠

Wednesday morning

2 Samuel 12. 1–7a, 13–23

Nathan catches the conscience of the king, David, with a story of intrigue similar to that which David was involved in. Nathan says to David, 'You are the man!'

Acts 14. 19–end

Paul is stoned, and dragged out of Iconium. With Barnabas, he makes his courageous way, 'throwing open the gates of faith to the Gentiles'.

*

Wednesday evening

Esther 4. 1–14

Haman's evil plot against the Jews is discovered by Mordecai who, in his duties, looks for ways of warning King Ahasuerus of it. Esther is to be the means of salvation. 'Who knows whether it is not for a time like this that you have become queen?'

2 Corinthians 12. 19–end

It is the behaviour of the Corinthian Christians which troubles Paul, and leads to great anxiety about how things will be when they meet.

✠

Thursday morning

2 Samuel 15. 13–23, 30

The dual kingship of David and Absalom causes David great grief, and he weeps as Jesus was to do later, on the Mount of Olives.

'My tears have been my food day and night' (Ps. 42.3).

Acts 15. 1–6

Fierce dissension between 'some from Judaea' on the one hand, and Paul and Barnabas on the other, over the matter of circumcision, splits the Church.

*

Thursday evening

Esther 5

The King has promised Esther whatever she wants and she requests two banquets, with Haman present at each. Haman is pleased at the special treatment but is still frustrated by the Jew, Mordecai's, presence at the court.

2 Corinthians 13. 1–4

The running store in the relationship between Paul and the Corinthian church leads Paul to liken his position to Christ's, who appeared weak, but was in fact strong in the power of God.

Friday morning

2 Samuel 16. 5–14

Shimei, one of Saul's family, throws stones and curses at David, but David responds stoically in order to gain the Lord's blessing.

'If anyone slaps you on the right cheek, turn and offer him the other also' (Matt. 5.38).

Acts 15. 7–21

On the question of the status of the Gentiles, Peter, Paul and Barnabas convince James, leader of the Judaean group, of the prophetic basis for the inclusion of the Gentiles in the household of faith.

*

Friday evening

Esther 6

An ironic twist occurs in the story, as Haman is asked by the King how he would honour someone. Assuming it is himself that is being referred to, he makes an elaborate list, only to discover it is Mordecai who is to be honoured.

2 Corinthians 13. 5–end

Paul wants the Corinthian church to live in peace, setting a good example of living peacably with each other. He concludes this section of the letter with the Grace.

'The grace of our Lord Jesus Christ,
and the love of God,
and the fellowship of the Holy Spirit,
be with you all.'

✠

Saturday morning

2 Samuel 17. 1–7, 11–22

Absalom, pursuing David, gets two different pieces of advice. The one from Hushai seems to be part of a fifth-column activity to help King David.

Acts 15. 22–35

As a result of these discussions, a letter is to be sent with Paul and Barnabas to the church at Antioch, allaying their fears on the need of maintain the strict rules of Judaism. Barnabas and Paul gave up their lives to the cause of their Lord Jesus Christ (v. 26).

✳

Saturday evening

Esther 7

Esther asks that her people be spared from the threat of extermination. King Ahasuerus discovers it is Haman who is trying to get rid of the Jews, and as a result Haman is executed on the gallows he had prepared for Mordechai.

Romans 1. 1–7

The letter, says Paul, is about Jesus Christ, our Lord. Karl Barth's great *Commentary* (1928) begins, 'The man who is now speaking is an emissary, bound to perform his duty.'

✠

WEEKDAYS FOLLOWING THE SEVENTH SUNDAY AFTER PENTECOST

Monday morning

2 Samuel 18. 1–17

Against the wishes of David, Absalom is killed in battle. He first got caught in a tree in the forest of Ephron and then a mob of ten, armour-bearers of Joab, killed him.

Acts 15. 36–40

Paul and Barnabas split over the decision to let John Mark accompany them. Barnabas goes with John Mark and Paul with Silas.

*

Monday evening

Ecclesiasticus 1. 1–10

The primacy of wisdom, and its feminine nature, is set out from the beginning of the work.

Romans 1. 8–17

Declaring the gospel is Paul's primary missionary motive. The gospel is the saving power of God for all, both Jew and Gentile.

Tuesday morning

2 Samuel 18. 19–end

The news of Absalom's death is brought to David. His lament from the roof-chamber over the gate echoes through time.

Acts 15.41 – 16.5

Paul meets Timothy at Lystra. The growth of the Church is very much a matter of people influencing people.

*

Tuesday evening

Ecclesiasticus 1. 11–21

To receive wisdom we need to stand in awe of God. Wisdom, far from being a dry academic thing, flourishes, gladdens, nourishes.

'To fear the Lord is the fulness of wisdom' (v. 16, RV).

Romans 1. 18–25

There is that in all people which can respond to God, but some refuse to honour God, worshipping the creation rather than the creator.

Wednesday morning

2 Samuel 19. 1–15

The victory of the army under Joab has taken second place to David's grief. Joab reports the disappointment of the people at this neglect of the army's success. David's private and public life are in conflict.

Acts 16. 6–15

The dramatic call of Paul to Macedonia is acted on, and there he meets Lydia who is baptized and offers hospitality.

Lord, come and stay at my house.

*

Wednesday evening

Ecclesiasticus 1. 22–end

Anger and arrogance easily take hold, without the restraint of wisdom.

Lord, help me to be truthful.

Romans 1. 26–end

The natural and the unnatural are being reversed. Paul is very strong indeed in his criticism of this.

Lord, help me to work along the grain of my own true nature.

Thursday morning

2 Samuel 24. 2, 9–24a

David's public and private lives here come together with the public census, and the private sense of guilt and foolishness.

Acts 16. 16–24

At Philippi, Paul and his companion Silas are put in prison for silencing the slave-girl possessed by a spirit of divination.

Thursday evening

Ecclesiasticus 2. 1–11

Faithfulness, even under the pressure of suffering, is the recommended path, in the way that gold is tried in the fire.

Romans 2. 1–11

Beware how you judge others. God is the judge, and he judges fairly, with no favourites, on the basis of individual conduct.

Friday morning

1 Kings 1. 28–40

Solomon succeeds David as king at David's request. The earth splits with the noise of rejoicing, which echoes forward to the death of Christ and the beginning of his reign, which was also announced by the breaking open of the earth.

Acts 16. 25–end

This is the moving story of the conversion and baptism of Paul's jailer. To his question, 'What must I do to be saved?' Paul replies, 'Put your trust in the Lord Jesus, and you will be saved.'

*

Friday evening

Ecclesiasticus 3. 17–29

Humility is the task of the great. To the humble God reveals his secrets.

Lord, help me to be humble, so that I may learn the secrets of your great love.

Romans 2. 12–24

Divisions occur in Paul's thought, according to how people stand in relation to the law. There are two laws: the Mosaic law, and the law written on the human heart.

O Lord, my heart is open to you.

✠

Saturday morning

1 Chronicles 22. 5–end

To Solomon, 'man of peace', is given the responsibility and the resources for building the Temple. The irony of all the talk of peace is not lost on those who reflect on the future history of the Temple.

Acts 17. 1–9

Jason, who had been looking after Paul and Silas in Thessalonica, is overrun by the mob and brought before the magistrate. Paul's proclamation continues the same: 'The Messiah had to suffer and rise from the dead.'

Saturday evening

Ecclesiasticus 4. 11–28

There is a right humility and a right sense of acknowledging your own abilities. Wisdom will help you decide.

Romans 2. 25–end

Another principle other than the external human law has its power over us, and that is the inner feelings of the heart, derived from and directed towards God.

✠

WEEKDAYS FOLLOWING THE EIGHTH SUNDAY AFTER PENTECOST

Monday morning

1 Chronicles 28. 1–10

King David's military life has not equipped him to be a builder of the Temple: this task is to be given to Solomon, his son, to perform. David's advice to his son is, 'If you search for God, he will let you find him'.

Acts 17. 10–15

The Jews of Beroea under Paul's influence study the scriptures every day to see whether what he was saying was true. Such eagerness to trawl the scriptures!

'Incline my heart to your decrees' (Ps. 119.36).

*

Monday evening

Ecclesiasticus 5. 1–8

Among the 'do not's' is this more positive note:

'Turn back to the Lord without delay
and do not defer action from one day to the
next' (v. 7).

Romans 3. 1–8

The sort of questions that the Jews might put – and Paul would understand this – are tests of God, rather than an entering into God's righteousness.

✠

Tuesday morning

1 Kings 2. 1–12

David gives his final word to Solomon, which has a strongly political flavour to it. He hands on his anxieties for his son, who he knows has greater wisdom, to deal with.

Acts 17. 16–end

Paul addresses the men of Athens, high up on a rock near the Parthenon. He speaks to cultured men of the need to repent, because they will soon be judged.

'What you worship but do not know – this is what I now proclaim' (v. 23).

*

Tuesday evening

Ecclesiasticus 6. 14–31

Wisdom is personified and acclaimed. 'You will put her on like a splendid robe' (v. 31).

Romans 3. 9–20

'Sin' on the part of the human race and righteousness on the part of God is the gulf which the letter sets itself to describe. The law has, in part, forged that gulf.

Wednesday morning

Ecclesiasticus 47. 2–11

A hymn to David the hymn writer, a poem for David the poet: 'In all he did he gave thanks'.

Acts 18. 1–11

In Corinth Paul stays with his fellow tentmaker, Aquila, and while he is there he is encouraged in his work by the Holy Spirit.

'Daughters of Jerusalem, I am dark and lovely,
like the tents of Kedar
or the tent curtains of Shalmah' (S. of S. 1.5).

*

Wednesday evening

Ecclesiasticus 7. 27–end

Such wisdom – good, dependable, sound wisdom! Reflect for a moment on the context out of which such wisdom must have come.

Romans 3. 21–26

Faith looks up to grace coming down, and all is made possible through Jesus Christ, who shows us that God is a forgiving God.

✠

Thursday morning

1 Kings 3. 4–14

Solomon's dream at Gibeon is of God asking him for what he wanted. Solomon asks for wisdom, and God is pleased.

'Grant your servant … a heart with skill to listen, so that he may … distinguish good from evil' (v. 9).

'I remember your name in the night, O Lord, and dwell upon your law' (Ps. 119.55).

Acts 18. 12–17

Gallio, proconsul of Achaia, is impatient with the complaints by the Jews against Paul. He has better things to do with his time.

✳

Thursday evening

Ecclesiasticus 10. 6–8, 12–25

The fear of the Lord is the answer to much that goes wrong as a result of neglecting the Lord.

Romans 3. 27–end

Faith, because it is uncheckable, has no tally for pride, whereas the law is much loved by those who need to succeed, and feared by those who fail.

✠

Friday morning

1 Kings 5. 1–12

The cedars of Lebanon are felled and floated to Solomon for the building of the Temple. Hiram, King of Tyre, and benefactor, acclaims this son of David for the wise rule of his people.

'The trees of the Lord are full of sap,
the cedars of Lebanon which he planted'
(Ps. 104.17).

Acts 18. 18–23

The vow to have his hair cut off is a rare window on to the particularity of Paul's personal life. He is moving around a lot: Cenchreae, Syria, Ephesus, Caeserea, Antioch, Phrygia.

✳

Friday evening

Ecclesiasticus 14.20 – 15.10

Wisdom is the mother and the beloved, who we are encouraged to stay close to.

Romans 4. 1–8

Abraham is the first mountain to cross on our journey of understanding faith, and before setting out on the climb we must understand God's act of 'counting' this faith, accepting it, as righteousness.

Saturday morning

1 Kings 8. 1–13

Solomon builds the Temple and the glory of the Lord fills it.

'Let Israel rejoice in his maker;
let the children of Zion be joyful in their king'
(Ps. 149.2).

Acts 18. 24–end

The Alexandrian, Apollos, a Jew who had begun to proclaim Jesus as Messiah, is having a great effect on the people of Ephesus.

*

Saturday evening

Ecclesiasticus 15. 11–end

The choice between sin and the fear of God, fire and water, death and life, is clearly set out.

Romans 4. 9–17

Abraham, the father of faith, was uncircumcised when his faith was counted to him for righteousness, and therefore, for Paul, is the 'patron saint' of Gentiles.

'God put Abraham to the test. "Abraham!" he called to him, and Abraham replied, "Here I am!" ' (Gen. 22.1)

WEEKDAYS FOLLOWING THE NINTH SUNDAY AFTER PENTECOST

Monday morning

1 Kings 8. 22–30

Solomon's extended prayer in the Temple has, with its rhetorical asides – 'Can God indeed dwell on earth?' – the form of a meditation on the presence of God among us.

'… and he shall be called Emmanuel, a name which means "God is with us" ' (Matt. 1.23).

Acts 19. 1–7

Paul is teaching the basics of the new way to the small number of disciples in Ephesus: about the Holy Spirit and about baptism in the name of Jesus.

Monday evening

Ecclesiasticus 17. 1–14

Echoing the creation story of Genesis, the writer summarizes God's gifts to human beings, their duties and their joys.

Romans 4. 16–end

The question, what is suitable faith, and what 'counts', affects us too. Acceptable faith is faith in God, who raised Christ Jesus from the dead.

Tuesday morning

1 Kings 10. 1–10

The Queen of Sheba comes to Solomon in person to confirm his reputation for wisdom.

'May there be given to him gold from Arabia' (Ps. 72.15).

Acts 19. 8–20

A distinction was being made between the true use of the name of Jesus in exorcisms, and a false use. Even the evil spirits themselves recognized the difference.

Tuesday evening

Ecclesiasticus 18. 1–14

In proportion to the greatness of God, human beings are very small, and that is why God shows his compassion to them.

Romans 5. 1–11

The 'then' of despair is replaced by the 'now' of hope and the glory to come. Christ's death for the wicked is a sign of God's love, and was the crucial turning point in the relationship between humanity and God.

Wednesday morning

1 Kings 11. 4–13

Solomon's unfaithfulness to God issues in God's wrenching the kingdom from his descendants, only leaving them Jerusalem.

Acts 19. 21–end

One important effect that the growth of the Christian community was having in Ephesus was its challenge to the cult of Artemis, and the financial implications of this caused a revolt.

Lord of all truth, teach us not to make a God of earthly things, but to worship you, the one Lord.

Wednesday evening

Ecclesiasticus 19. 13–end

The truth of a person is not always easily observed. Although the outward appearance gives clues, the truth often lies deeper.

'Alas! ... You clean the outside of a cup or a dish, and leave the inside full of greed and self-indulgence!' (Matt. 23.25)

Romans 5. 12–end

'Grace' is the word Paul uses to describe the action of God in neutralizing the power of sin. Grace is summed up in the death of Jesus, God's great saving act of grace.

Thursday morning

1 Kings 11. 26–40

The split between the twelve tribes is the subject of a prophecy to Jeroboam by Abijah: ten to Jeroboam, and Jerusalem to remain for David's descendants. So Israel and Judah are destined to be set apart.

Acts 20. 1–6

The journey continues, described by Luke, one of the travelling companions. Paul is still meeting with aggressive persecution from the Jews.

*

Thursday evening

Ecclesiasticus 21. 11–end

Wisdom and foolishness are shown in action.

Romans 6. 1–11

Sin is over for those who have been baptized. Sin died for us as we shared the death of Christ. Life begins 'in union with Christ Jesus'.

Friday morning

1 Kings 12. 1–19

Fathers and sons. Rehoboam the son of Solomon is in the grip of the Lord's prophecy to his father, and the inevitable split between Judah and Israel begins to open.

Acts 20. 7–16

The young man Eutychus falls out of the window with drowsiness, but is declared by the preacher Paul to be alive.

*

Friday evening

Ecclesiasticus 22. 6–22

Foolishness is a heavy weight. To help us understand we have images of a house, and a fence on a hilltop, interspersed with a description of friendship.

Romans 6. 12–14

The choice is still ours, and we must choose the way of life, to put ourselves at the disposal of God.

Saturday morning

1 Kings 12. 26–32

Jeroboam felt the need to set up his own centres of worship at Bethel and Dan, and employed non-levitical priests. 'This … became a sin in Israel' (v. 30).

Acts 20. 17–end

Paul's departure from Miletus and his farewell address to the Christians there conveys all the toughness and the heartfelt quality of the man, as well as people's great affection for him. Farewells on the quay stretch back in their resonance to the first adventurers.

*

Saturday evening

Ecclesiasticus 22.27 – 23.15

The tongue is a cause of downfall. The sins that come from the lips and from talk are vividly described.

'Keep your tongue from evil-speaking
and your lips from lying words' (Ps. 34.13).

Romans 6. 15–end

Holiness is leading a life apart from sin, and in union with Christ Jesus.

'In the beauty of holiness have I begotten you, like dew from the womb of the morning' (Ps. 110.3).

✠

WEEKDAYS FOLLOWING THE TENTH SUNDAY AFTER PENTECOST

Monday morning

1 Kings 13. 1–10

A man of God from Judah inveighs against the sanctuary at Bethel and shows God's power over Jeroboam.

O nameless man of God, so powerful in healing, and strong in obedience to God.

Acts 21. 1–14

The travel, the preaching, the hospitality are familiar scenes of Paul's preaching journeys. Into this comes the prophetic action of Agabus.

*

Monday evening

Ecclesiasticus 24. 1–22

In a particular place, in the place that God chooses, wisdom is found and nurtured. Once found it produces great beauty.

Lord, help me find my place, and to know my place is where I am with you.

Romans 7. 1–6

Death as a way of life only makes sense as a death to the old way of life, a way which was dominated by sin.

✠

Tuesday morning

1 Kings 17. 1–16

Elijah is fed by ravens and drinks from the stream. In a severe drought he miraculously provides food for the widow of Zarephath.

Elijah, pray for us.

Acts 21. 15–26

Paul arrives in Jerusalem and enters the tense situation of the relation of Jew to Gentile. James asks for compromise from Paul.

*

Tuesday evening

Ecclesiasticus 24. 23–end

The book of the covenant is the source of wisdom; it pours out like a great river.

Romans 7. 7–13

Law must be distinguished from sin. Law highlights sin, and gives greater opportunity for that death which becomes new life.

Wednesday morning

1 Kings 17. 17–end

Elijah restores the widow's son to life. The compassion, power and control of Elijah are a prelude to the healing ministry of Jesus.

'Love children especially' (Dostoyevsky).

Acts 21. 27–40a

The ancitipated turmoil occurs in Jerusalem, ignited by the Jews who are threatened by Paul's reforms.

Wednesday evening

Ecclesiasticus 27.30 – 28.9

Anger destroys wisdom. Forgiveness is the fruit of wisdom.

Romans 7. 14–end

The ordinary human motives are in conflict with another, better way. From this impasse only God can release us.

'Who is there to rescue me from this state of death! Who but God? Thanks be to him through Jesus Christ our Lord!' (vv. 24, 25)

✠

Thursday morning

1 Kings 18. 20–39

In the contest between Elijah and the worshippers of Baal, the Lord God proves his power by the burning up of the whole offering and all the apparatus of the altar. Elijah's prayer is a classic one.

'Lord God of Abraham, of Isaac, and of Israel, let it be known today that you are God in Israel and that I am your servant' (v. 36).

Acts 21.40b – 22.21

Paul tells the Jews in Jerusalem the story of his conversion.

⁎

Thursday evening

Ecclesiasticus 35. 1–12

The art of giving, or offering, is described in all its subtlety, freed from its narrow levitical constraints.

Romans 8. 1–11

Spirituality is here fleshed out: it is Paul's teaching about the place of the Holy Spirit as it gives life.

'Those who live on the level of the spirit have the spiritual outlook, and that is life and peace' (v. 6).

✠

Friday morning

1 Kings 18. 41–end

Elijah's prophetic activity is combined with an acute concentration on the weather. Elijah is much involved with Ahab's rule and its success. The rains would make the dirt roads impassable.

There are some times, O God, when I need to tuck up my robe and run before you.

Acts 22. 22–29

The Jews take offence at Paul and he is taken into custody. Just before he is beaten, he declares his Roman citizenship.

✳

Friday evening

Ecclesiasticus 36. 1–5, 10–17

A prayer to God by those who faithfully belong to him and seek for courage and guidance.

Romans 8. 12–17

The Spirit helps us relate as spiritual children to a spiritual parent.

✠

Saturday morning

1 Kings 19. 1–16

Elijah, the contemplative, calls on God. Elijah is distressed but hears the Lord in the still, small voice.

Waiting for God, patiently, quietly, gently …

Acts 22.30 – 23.11

Paul addresses the Jewish Council, rather as Jesus did, but Paul's stinging tongue lashes out and he cleverly sets the Pharisees against the Sadducees.

*

Saturday evening

Ecclesiasticus 37. 7–15

Advice is a valuable commodity, and you need to ask for it from the appropriate person, particularly the God-fearing.

Romans 8. 18–30

The communication between God and us is directed by the Spirit, even if it seems to us like inarticulate groans.

'Let the words of my mouth and the
meditation of my heart
be acceptable in your sight,
O Lord, my strength and my redeemer'
(Ps. 19.14)

WEEKDAYS FOLLOWING THE ELEVENTH SUNDAY AFTER PENTECOST

Monday morning

1 Kings 21. 1–16

Such sinister dealings, which have the darkness and horror of *Macbeth*, reveal to us the depth of greed of Ahab and Jezebel and the violence to Naboth this greed gives rise to.

O Lord, help me to see the danger of greed.

Acts 23. 12–22

A cabal of Jews have sworn not to eat or drink until Paul is killed. Paul's nephew hears of this and is instrumental in helping his uncle.

*

Monday evening

Ecclesiasticus 38. 24–end

To everyone their talent, and in the perfecting of their talent is their prayer: smith, potter, craft worker. The scholar in the same way pursues wisdom, and needs to concentrate on that.

Knowing my gift, let me give time to it, and so praying through it, give glory to God.

'As kingfishers catch fire, dragonflies draw flame; ... Each mortal thing does one thing and the same' (Gerard Manley Hopkins).

Romans 8. 31–end

Love is the pivotal point of this passage: 'victory is ours through him who loved us'. Despite suffering, the love of Christ sustains us. We are inseparable from Christ because of it.

'O love that will not let me go ...'

✠

Tuesday morning

1 Kings 21. 17–end

Elijah reproves Ahab in the strongest terms possible, prophesying destruction for Ahab and Jezebel.

O Lord, give me courage to speak out against evil.

Acts 23. 23–end

So like Jesus in his trials, Paul is shunted from court to court.

Pray for all hostages, and for those held in prison for their beliefs.

Tuesday evening

Ecclesiasticus 39. 1–11

Set apart are those who devote themselves to reflecting on the law of the Most High. This is a beautiful description of the spiritual life.

Lord, let me delight to be one whose study is your way, your word, your will.

Romans 9. 1–5

Paul celebrates his roots in the traditions of Judaism, his kinsfolk by natural descent.

✠

Wednesday morning

1 Kings 22. 29–end

The dramatic defeat of Ahab in his chariot is the fulfilment of the prophecy which came from his killing of Naboth. The dogs licked the blood from the floor of the chariot at the prostitutes' well at Samaria.

'The evil that men do lives after them' (William Shakespeare).

Acts 24. 1–9

Tertullus, accompanied by Ananias, opens the case against Paul, in the presence of Felix, the Governor.

✳

Wednesday evening

Ecclesiasticus 42. 15–end

A thoughtful hymn on the works God's word has made.

Romans 9. 6–13

Searching for spiritual, not natural, connections with the line of Abraham, Paul links the faith of Abraham with its fulfilment in Christ.

✠

Thursday morning

2 Kings 1. 3–16

Elijah challenges Ahaziah, the King of Samaria, over his involvement with Baal-zebub. He brings down fire from heaven on Ahaziah's army and messengers.

Acts 24. 10–21

Paul is given the chance to reply to the governor; and he says that he has given no cause for objection, even though he is a supporter of the 'new way'.

∗

Thursday evening

Ecclesiasticus 43. 13–26

Snowstorm, thunder, south wind, winter weather, scorching heat followed by refreshing dew, and the planting of islands in the deep, form a litany of some of God's creative work.

'... and by his word all things consist' (Ecclus. 43.26, RV).

Romans 9. 14–24

The primacy of God's will is the guiding notion here, as the potter's is over the pots, to be made or destroyed; or, as in this case, to be loved because of their flaws.

Friday morning

2 Kings 2. 1–15

Elijah will hand his spirit over to Elisha on the understanding that Elisha sees him go. Elisha does indeed see him go, ascending, surrounded by chariots of fire and in a whirlwind.

See Blake's pictures of this ascension.

Acts 24. 22–end

Paul is still in custody in Caesarea, but Felix the governor allows him to speak to Drusilla, his wife. Paul speaks about Christ Jesus, but when he talks of moral issues, Felix concludes the conversation.

'... but it seemed to me, she longed for Jesus Christ.'

(John Chrysostom, *Homilies on Acts*)

*

Friday evening

Ecclesiasticus 51. 1–12

In the middle of difficulty this prayer of thanksgiving bravely shines out with its bright rays.

'Begging to be rescued from death
I cried, "Lord, you are my Father" '
(51. 9b, 10a).

Romans 9. 25–end

God's love for the lonely and outcast extends to the Gentiles, whose rightness comes through faith not through law. The rock is the rock of stumbling and of faith.

'Some will believe and some still stumble. But stumbling comes from gaping after other things.'

(John Chrysostom, *Homilies on Romans*)

✠

Saturday morning

Ecclesiasticus 48. 1–14

A hymn to Elijah makes a fine and fitting memorial. He returns to be with Jesus on the mount of the transfiguration.

'Blessed are they that saw thee,
And they that have been beautified with love'
(Ecclus. 48.11, RV).

Acts 25. 1–12

Festus succeeds Felix as governor, and sides with the Jews against Paul. Paul keeps strong in his own defence and demands to see Caesar.

'Those who are my enemies without cause are mighty,
and many in number are those who wrongfully hate me' (Ps. 38.19).

*

Saturday evening

Ecclesiasticus 51. 13–end

Wisdom, as the great feminine quality of God, has been with the writer from the beginning of his journey, on through the process of study, and has issued in his life's work.

'I delight in your commandments
which I have always loved' (Ps. 119.47).

Romans 10. 1–4

Christ is the rock, the fulfilment of the law and the bringer of righteousness, for everyone who has faith.

Christ, my rock, my rule, my righteousness.

WEEKDAYS FOLLOWING THE TWELFTH SUNDAY AFTER PENTECOST

Monday morning

2 Kings 2. 15–22

The followers of Elijah and Elisha offer to look for the whereabouts of the departed Elijah. It is a reminder of Peter's request to Jesus to make three booths on the mount of transfiguration, fruitlessly to preserve the glory of the past.

Acts 25. 13–end

There is a sense here that the writer, Luke, is filling in a lot of background material about Roman justice. Paul is brought before Festus and King Agrippa.

'... someone called Jesus, a dead man whom Paul alleged to be alive' (v. 19).

*

Monday evening

Hosea 1. 2–8; 2.16 – 3 end

In an elaborate metaphor of God's relationship with Israel, Hosea proclaims Israel's unfaithfulness, through the prophetic act of marrying an unchaste woman. The restoration of the relationship is acknowledged by the making of a covenant.

Romans 10. 5–13

Lips and heart are the means of confessing 'Jesus is Lord'. Lips to speak it, heart to mean it. The reward is salvation.

'The word is near you' (v. 8).

*

Tuesday morning

2 Kings 4. 1–17

Elisha helps a widow pay her debts by the sale of miraculously flowing oil. He is offered an oratory at Shunem by a rich woman, which he accepts, and prophesies the birth of a child for her.

Acts 26. 1–23

The story of Paul's conversion is again described in Acts, this time as a defence by Paul for not disobeying a heavenly vision.

'The Messiah ... as the first to rise from the dead ... would announce the dawn' (v. 23).

After a long night of searching, the dayspring from on high visits us.

*

Tuesday evening

Hosea 5.15 – 6.6

First the Lord speaks, then Hosea, and then the Lord, and then Hosea speaks again. There are different voices, but an intimate connection between them. Faith in the middle of rejection brings resurrection.

'After two days he will revive us,
on the third day he will raise us' (6.2).

Romans 10. 14–end

The communication of the good news needs its communicators, and yet, as Isaiah knew, God anticipates all human desire to hear.

'How beautiful are the feet of those who bring good news!' (v. 15, NIV)

✠

Wednesday morning

2 Kings 4. 18–37

Elisha on Mount Carmel is called to Shunem to revive the child. He does this by lying over the child, and warming him. So we proportion ourselves spiritually to others' souls to heal them.

Acts 26. 24–end

Paul, in chains, longs for people, high and low, Jew and Gentile, to accept that Jesus of Nazareth is the Messiah.

'King Agrippa, do you believe the prophets?' (v. 27)

Help me to see and feel the anointed nature of Jesus, his unique closeness to God the Father.

*

Wednesday evening

Hosea 8. 4–14

Samaria, Israel and Ephraim are the objects of Hosea's fiercest attacks. All of them in one way or another reject the Lord God, failing to understand that he is not made or fabricated, but is the law-giver and the punisher of sin.

Romans 11. 1–10

A question mark hangs over the love of God towards Israel. The idea of the holy remnant, and the hardness of heart of the people towards God, are fully documented in the Old Testament.

'However hard you listen, you will never understand.
However hard you look, you will never perceive' (Isa. 6.8).

✠

Thursday morning

2 Kings 5. 1–19a

A young and nameless girl leads Naaman, who had leprosy, to Elisha. The medicine of dipping seven times in the River Jordan asks for humility from the great commander, and issues in his praising the Lord God.

'Wash and be clean' (v. 13).

Lord, help me to accept the simple things in humility, for my healing.

Acts 27. 1–8

Paul, with some other passengers, is taken by Julius the centurion to Rome. The boat journey is charted by Luke with great drama and detail.

Pray with a map open in front of you ...

Thursday evening

Hosea 10. 1–12

Things don't change: injustice, adultery, the setting up of sacred calves. Success and wealth mean more dependence on merely human show.

'Sow justice, and reap loyalty' (v. 12).

Romans 11. 11–16

In the end nothing is lost. All is a part of God's providential care. The Jew and the Gentile, both will be a living example of life from the dead.

'If the first loaf is holy, so is the whole batch' (v. 16).

'All shall be well,' said Julian of Norwich,
all manner of thing shall be well.

Friday morning

2 Kings 6. 8–23

The King of Aram is skirmishing with the King of Israel, while Elisha, in the middle, manipulates an Israelite victory.

O Lord, help me to see what Elisha saw, that there are more on our side than on theirs, and that through our faith in you, we are surrounded by invisible chariots of fire.

Acts 27. 9–20

A storm at sea off Crete hits the boat, with Paul and Luke on board. The boat set sail against Paul's advice.

'Three times I have been shipwrecked ...' (2 Cor. 11.25).

*

Friday evening

Hosea 11. 1–9a

The radical personalization of God leads God to swings of temperament, from anger to pity, from judgement to forgiveness. Hosea uses his experience as father and husband and widower, young man and old, to penetrate the feelings of God, and yet he also hears God say:

'I am God, not a mortal' (v. 9).

Romans 11. 17–24

Paul uses the picture of grafting olive branches to say that the Gentiles are the grafted branches, and the Jews the parent stock. The root gives sap to both, but there is no place for pride.

'Observe the kindness and the severity of God' (v. 22).

Jesus said: 'I am the vine; you are the branches' (John 15.5).

Saturday morning

2 Kings 6.24 – 7. 7, 16

We have to imagine minor skirmishes in an extended campaign, one of which was remembered for the day some Israelites escaped the siege to find the Aramaean camp deserted.

Acts 27. 21–26

Paul calms the fear of the travellers with the assurance that God would save them.

'... the God whose I am and whom I worship ...' (v. 23)

Help me to take heart.

*

Saturday evening

Hosea 14. 2–end

Here is a vision of hope and forgiveness, restoration, new life, coming back, a return to God.

'Come back to the Lord
with your words of confession' (v. 2).

Romans 11. 25–32

Paul searches the scriptures for his understanding of God. Here he lights on the 'deliverer'. Paul's mind also delights in balances and counterweights, which are reconciled by Christ.

WEEKDAYS FOLLOWING THE THIRTEENTH SUNDAY AFTER PENTECOST

Monday morning

2 Kings 9. 1–13

The destruction of the House of Ahab takes its relentless way through the initiative of Elisha. By means of one of his school of prophets, Jehu is anointed king at Ramoth-gilead.

'You will be brought before governors and kings on my account' (Matt. 10.18).

Acts 27. 27–38

Here is a mixture of dramatic action at sea, and hints of a carefully crafted mixing of the life of Paul with that of Jesus.

'Let us keep the saints with us,' said John Chrysostom, 'and there will be no tempest. Paul is sailing even now with us.'

*

Monday evening

Joel 1. 1–15

A scene of devastation among the crops of the harvest is a prelude to the coming of the Lord. The terror affects all levels of society.

'... The day of the Lord: it comes' (v. 15).

Guard us waking, guard us sleeping.

Romans 11. 33–end

This is a paeon of praise that strikes inwards – 'how deep' – rather than upwards. Paul and Job sing together. The unfathomable mind of the Lord has to be put on.

'From him and through him and for him all things exist' (v. 36).

Lord Jesus Christ, only you can help me do the impossible.

Tuesday morning

2 Kings 9. 14–26

Jehoram, son of Ahab, takes the full brunt of his father's guilt, and is killed by Jehu.

Acts 27. 39–end

Abandon ship: there was nothing else for it. A strange impersonal tone creeps into the final verses. How did Paul and Luke get on in the sea?

'Consider what a thing it is', said John Chrysostom, 'to have a holy man in the house.'

*

Tuesday evening

Joel 2. 1–2, 10–17

A real warning of the judgement comes with its escape route: penance, fasting, prayer.

Let me repent of my evil.

'Rend your hearts and not your garments' (v. 13).

Romans 12. 1–8

Human conduct as it washes the shore of the divine; the total transformation of our minds as they direct our behaviour; and all this is set in the context of humbly fitting in with others.

I implore you, Lord, to help me by your grace to offer my very self to you.

Wednesday morning

2 Kings 9. 27–end

All that is left of Jezebel after she is thrown from the window in Jezreel, are the palms of her hands.

O Israel, the purity of your faith took a long time to be born, through all the struggles and murders of kings. So it is with my soul.

Acts 28. 1–10

The Malta days were remembered for Paul's power against a viper, and the healing of Publius' father, and for the peace, calm and welcome that the islanders gave them.

'Paul visited him and, after prayer, laid his hands on him and healed him' (v. 8).

Wednesday evening

Joel 2. 21–end

This is a dramatic and extreme scenario. It is black and white, all or nothing, doom, or rejoicing in the great and terrible day of the Lord.

Lord, have mercy.

Romans 12. 9–end

This is the Christian character, the image of God in human behaviour.

'If your enemy is hungry, feed him' (v. 20).

✠

Thursday morning

2 Kings 10. 18–28

Because of his fierce hatred of Baal worship, Jehu tricks the ministers of Baal into a massacre.

Acts 28. 11–16

And so to Rome: a wonderful meeting with fellow Christians, after a long and traumatic journey.

'When Paul saw [the Christians there], he gave thanks to God and took courage' (v. 15).

'Distinguish the Rome of the Caesars', says Thomas Merton, 'from the Rome of the martyrs.'

✳

Thursday evening

Joel 3. 11–end

Much of this imagery of the end of things is taken up by Jesus in his teachings. There is a lovely description of the fruitfulness of Jerusalem as the centrepiece of hope on that day.

Lord, make me ready.

'When that day comes …
a fountain will spring from the Lord's house' (v. 18).

Romans 13. 1–7

The debate about law and love is fuelled by this passage which says so much. Law on the whole helps us, but love saves us.

'If love leaves us the whole body is rent in pieces' (Lancelot Andrewes).

'O Lord, grant to our powerful men to have no power against the truth, but for the truth' (Lancelot Andrewes).

✠

Friday morning

2 Kings 11. 1–18

Ahaziah causes all male contenders to the throne of David to be massacred. Joash, hidden in the Temple precinct by Jehosheba, escapes.

Hide me, O Lord, under the shadow of your wings.

Acts 28. 17–22

Paul is clear that his progress through the courts is as a result of the Jews' determination to convict him. Paul is equally adamant that he is working for the ultimate benefit of the Jews.

'It is for loyalty to the hope of Israel that I am in these chains' (v. 20).

*

Friday evening

Malachi 1. 1–11

In dialogue form, the Lord is challenged by a recalcitrant Israel to show how he has loved them. Greater love seems to come from the 'nations' beyond Israel.

'From farthest east to farthest west,
my name is great among the nations' (v. 11).

Romans 13. 8–end

The ten commandments are summed up in the rule of love. So there is no rule but the rule of love, and no debt but the debt of love.

Christ Jesus, be the armour that I wear.

✠

Saturday morning

2 Chronicles 24. 17–25

The destiny of King Joash is described. He killed Zechariah, the son of Jehoida the High Priest, yet it was Jehoida who had given sanctuary to Joash when he was a young child.

Acts 28. 23–end

The final section of Acts has Paul repeating to himself the famous ironic indictment of Isaiah towards his people, for failing to grasp or understand what is before their eyes.

Open my eyes that I may see more clearly.

*

Saturday evening

Malachi 2. 1–12

A very strong word to priests is given about the need to be faithful to God, and not to lead the people astray.

'Men hang on the words of the priest and seek knowledge and instruction from him, because he is the messenger of the Lord of Hosts' (v. 7).

Romans 14. 1–12

As an antidote to arrogance and judging others, Paul appeals for a gentle sensitivity to another's way and needs.

Lord, help me not to be judgemental.

✠

WEEKDAYS FOLLOWING THE FOURTEENTH SUNDAY AFTER PENTECOST

Monday morning

2 Kings 17. 5–18

The by-now-familiar tale of disobedience to the Lord manifests itself in Baal worship. This leads to God's rejection of all except Judah.

Blessed are the pure in heart:
for they shall see God.

Titus 1. 1–4

Paul sets out his credentials at the beginning of this letter to Titus. Paul is an apostle through faith, knowledge and hope.

How would I describe my credentials?

*

Monday evening

Malachi 2.17 – 3.5

The crisis is near and a judgement impending. The Lord will look for purity from his priests and sound justice for the hired labourers and widows.

'... purified by either fire or fire ...' (T. S. Eliot)

Romans 14. 13–21

The practicalities of food regulations are important because they express the love of the neighbour, but they are not the most important thing.

'The kingdom of God is not eating or drinking, but justice, peace, and joy, inspired by the Holy Spirit' (v. 17).

Tuesday morning

2 Kings 19. 8–20, 35–end

Hezekiah, fearful of an Assyrian invasion, prays to the Lord.

'... that all the kingdoms of the earth may know that you alone, Lord, are God' (v. 19).

Lord, let me, like Hezekiah, spread my needs before you.

Titus 1. 5–end

Titus, left behind in Crete, is given advice on the quality of character needed in the elders of the church. They are to be 'unimpeachable' and 'blameless' (v. 6).

*

Tuesday evening

Malachi 3.13 – 4.2

Two distinct groups confront the law: those who are disgruntled and questioning God's power, and those who fear the Lord.

Lord, make us people for your own possession.

Romans 14.22 – 15.6

Rules for living together are inspired by Paul's longing for unity, based on personal convictions and commitment to scripture.

Let the scriptures be to me an instruction, an encouragement, the source of hope, and the means of perseverance.

✠

Wednesday morning

2 Kings 22. 8–end

The discovery of the scroll of the law by Hilkiah the High Priest and its being read by Josiah the King causes great heart-searching, and a new start to worshipping the Lord with greater devotion.

Titus 2. 1–10

Our lives well lived add lustre to the doctrine of God our Saviour. Here are nuggets of good advice, for the older and younger members of the community, and for husbands and wives.

*

Wednesday evening

Habbakuk 1. 1–11

Habbakuk is possessed with the violence of the world around him, and wonders what help the Lord is giving. He sees an answer in the imminent invasion of the land by the Chaldeans.

' "Violence!" I cry out to you,
but you do not come to the rescue' (v. 2).

Romans 15. 7–13

The ancient writings affirm Paul's mission to the Gentiles.

And may God, who is the ground of hope, fill me with all joy and peace as I lead the life of faith until, by the power of the Holy Spirit, I overflow with hope.

Thursday morning

2 Kings 23. 1–3, 15, 21–23

Josiah, in the presence of the entire population, renews the covenant with the Lord, and they keep Passover as it has never been kept before.

Eighteen years for the word of God, by chance discovery, to light up Josiah's love and obedience to God …

Titus 2. 11–end

The appeal to live a life of godliness in this present age speaks as strongly now as it did to Titus in Crete in the first century.

O Lord, that our living and our dying may be holy.

✳

Thursday evening

Habbakuk 1.12 – 2.4

The perplexity over the righteousness of God and the wickedness of the people is resolved by a vision of patient waiting for the appointed time.

Lord, my rock.

Romans 15. 14–21

Paul repeats to the Corinthian church that his prime concerns are with the Gentiles and with the centrality of Christ.

Centre me, O Lord, on you.

Friday morning

2 Kings 24. 8–17

Jehoiachin 'did what was wrong in the eyes of the Lord', and as a result the Babylonians under Nebuchadnezzar capture Jerusalem. The Temple is sacked, the people are deported, and the Exile begins.

Titus 3. 1–8a

The ancient spiritual wisdom of keeping clear of those who deal in arguments was to be picked up in the third century by the Desert Fathers.

✳

Friday evening

Habbakuk 3. 2–6, 16–end

God's great creative power extends to his judgements, and to the barrenness of nature.

'In your wrath you did not forget mercy' (v. 2).

Romans 15. 22–end

The plans Paul has in mind, he shares with his fellow Christians in Corinth. These include the project for raising funds.

Let your name, O Lord, be heard in all the earth.

Saturday morning

2 Kings 25. 1–12, 18–21

Zedekiah fought against the attacking Babylonians and was eventually overcome. Nebuchadnezzar had little mercy on him, his sons, or his council.

Titus 3. 8b–end

Good works nurture faith.

'… the good works you have prepared for me to walk in …'

*

Saturday evening

Nahum 1. 1–3, 3. 1–7, 18–end

Here is no story but stabs at understanding God's actions and his character which have so haunted Nahum.

'Bashan and Carmel languish,
and on Lebanon the young shoots wither'
(v. 4).

Romans 16. 17–end

Paul is winding up the letter with the usual remembrances to people, and final summary of his teaching.

Lord, help me to be expert in goodness, wise unto that which is good.

✠

WEEKDAYS IN WEEK 'A' (PENTECOST)

Monday morning

Proverbs 1. 8–19

Getting rich by illegal means is condemned.

'Thou shalt not steal' (Exod. 20.15, AV).

1 John 1. 1–4

Like the Gospel prologue, this letter begins with an over-arching summary of the faith. The reality, the physicality of the Word is placed centrally.

'... eternal life ... made visible' (v. 2).

O Lord, make my joy complete.

*

Monday evening

Zephaniah 1. 2–13

A more uncompromising and wholesale destruction could not be imagined as judgement by God on sin, and this is the news Zephaniah has to broadcast.

Matthew 4. 12–17

Jesus is living out the vision of Isaiah. The light is dawning in Galilee.

'The people that walked in darkness
have seen a great light' (Isa. 9.2).

✠

Tuesday morning

Proverbs 1. 20–end

Wisdom confronts insolence and prepares herself for withholding her gifts to those who have no fear of the Lord.

'Whoever listens to me will live …
undisturbed by fear' (v. 33).

1 John 1. 5–7

Light and darkness are the images John uses to give us a language to speak of the sense of God, or of his absence.

Lead us from darkness to light.
(From 'Prayer for Peace', adapted from the *Hindu Upanishads* by Satish Kumar.)

*

Tuesday evening

Zephaniah 1.14 – 2.3

The day of days will bring the great judgement of God. Nobody will escape, except maybe a few righteous and a handful of the humble.

'Seek the Lord … it may be that you will find shelter' (2.3).

Matthew 4. 18–end

Jesus gathers his first disciples, and begins with them his healing and teaching ministry.

'Come with me, and I will make you fishers of men' (v. 19).

'The splash of nets … the grind of sand and shell,
The boat hooks clash, the boat oars jar, the cries to buy and sell' (G. K. Chesterton).

✠

Wednesday morning

Proverbs 2. 1–9, 20–end

The value of wisdom is prized very highly. Like the Kingdom of Heaven, wisdom is buried treasure to be dug for.

Lord, grant me the wisdom of your prophets and saints, to discern and to counsel.

1 John 1.8 – 2.2

Sin is inevitable but redeemable.

O bone Jesus. O good Jesus.

'Hear what Saint John says:
If anyone sins, we have an advocate with the Father, Jesus Christ the righteous; and he is the propitiation for our sins' (ASB).

*

Wednesday evening

Zephaniah 3. 1–8

The tyrant city comes under severe judgement – its rulers, prophets, priests, and the arrogant people.

'Morning after morning he gives his judgement' (v. 5).

Often, Lord, I only think of your love; this will remind me of the sharp sword of your justice.

Matthew 5. 1–12

If this was all we had, it would be enough, but that enough would be very different from the values we know today. This is the ice-cold fresh water that comes right from the source.

'The Sermon on the Mount', said Mahatma Gandhi, 'went straight to my heart.'

Lord, help our structures to support the challenging truths of this teaching.

Thursday morning

Proverbs 3. 1–12

Wisdom is correction, and this needs to be understood as a necessary part of a process.

'Those whom the Lord loves he reproves' (v. 12).

1 John 2. 3–11

Living like Christ will be a walking in the light.

*

Thursday evening

Zephaniah 3. 9–13

The blessed remnant are like Jesus' 'blessed': the poor and lowly people who have no lying lips, nor are proud or arrogant.

'They will feed and lie down
with no one to terrify them' (v. 13).

Matthew 5. 13–19

We are salt, we are light, and moving from images into realities, we are bound by the law.

Friday morning

Proverbs 3. 13–26

Wisdom here equates with the enlightenment and awareness that Buddhism encourages. It is more than just a mental ability. It is a gift of the whole being.

'The Lord will be at your side,
and he will keep your feet from the trap'
(v. 26).

1 John 2. 12–17

John encourages us to shun and skirt what passes away but to pursue what continues for ever.

Lord, let my gaze be continually fixed on you.
Preserve me from attachments that bring no peace.

*

Friday evening

Zephaniah 3. 14–end

Into all the darkness of judgement, shine the lights of comfort and homecoming.

'When that time comes I shall gather you and bring you home' (v. 20).

Father of all … when we were still far off you met us in your Son and brought us home (ASB).

Matthew 5. 20–32

Our virtue, our holiness, and our obedience must begin in the secret places of the heart. That central home of the Spirit must be spotless.

Saturday morning

Proverbs 3. 27–end

The domestic world of getting along with those who live closest to you is sometimes the most important world.

'Love your neighbour as yourself' (Lev. 19.18).

1 John 2. 18–end

The importance of right belief, or giving glory to God, not antichrist, taxes John's mind. Dwelling in Christ is his surety.

*

Saturday evening

Obadiah 1. 1–14, 16–end

Edom, the traditional enemy of the Jews, stands condemned. Mount Zion will rise up from the land around, harbouring its holy remnant.

Matthew 5. 33–end

'Boundless', 'limitless' goodness is the ideal to which we are called. It is the impossible ethic which becomes possible the more we are with God.

'Love your enemies and pray for your persecutors' (Matt. 5.44).

Lord, I am cautious because I only see my own resources. Help me to be wholly yours.

✠

WEEKDAYS IN WEEK 'B' (PENTECOST)

Monday morning

Proverbs 4. 1–9

Wisdom, personified as feminine, is to be loved, cherished, embraced, and never forsaken.

Sancta Sophia, help me to be receptive to your gifts.

1 John 3. 1–10

Sin is acting against the will of God. To know God is to love him and to act righteously. Knowing God is to live in his pure atmosphere in which 'sin' is unthinkable.

'Me thoughts I heard one calling, Child!
And I reply'd, My Lord!'
(George Herbert, 'The Collar')

*

Monday evening

Song of Solomon 1.12 – 2.7

In the language of human desire, we reflect on our love of God, and God's love for us.

'Mary took a pound of costly ointment of pure nard and anointed the feet of Jesus and wiped his feet with her hair; and the house was filled with the fragrance of the ointment' (John 12.3, RSV).

Matthew 6. 1–4

Secrecy and humility are of the essence in our generosity. To parade our charity is to cancel the gift itself.

Tuesday morning

Proverbs 4. 10–end

The intensity of the moral voice here makes us wonder about its provenance and its effect. It rests heavily for its imagery on walking in the way, and links up with the Gospel images of the narrow way, and Jesus saying, 'I am the way'.

Guide me towards you,
guard my lips because of you,
fix my gaze upon you.

1 John 3. 11–end

Conscience is the pivot on which our judgements turn. Love is the power that unites us with Christ.

*

Tuesday evening

Song of Solomon 2. 8–end

The urgency of the relationship, and the energy it engenders, give a picture of love in its depth and great breadth.

'Hark! My beloved! Here he comes, bounding over the mountains, leaping over the hills' (v. 8).

Matthew 6. 5–15

Prayer should be brief, and secret. The Lord's Prayer is a summary of Jesus' teaching and a glimpse into his innermost thoughts.

Abba, Father, not my will, but yours, be done.

Wednesday morning

Proverbs 5. 1–14

With overtones of the morality play, the character Adultery is vividly portrayed as a warning to us.

'Thou shalt not commit adultery' (Exod. 20.14, AV).

Lord, lead me not into temptation.

1 John 4. 1–6

Does the spirit acknowledge Jesus? That is the test of truth. It is as simple and profound as that.

'I believe in Jesus Christ, God's only Son' (Lancelot Andrewes).

Lord, I believe, help my unbelief.

*

Wednesday evening

Song of Solomon 3

Timing is of the essence. God's time: … 'until I had brought him to my mother's house … until it is ready … his sword ready at his side against the terrors of the night.' All leads up to the wedding day, on which the banquet will have strange echoes of the Kingdom banquet of Jesus' parables.

Matthew 6. 16–24

Fasting and money are very real, practical things. The Sermon on the Mount deals in realities, but light and darkness come as an imaginative interlude.

Thursday morning

Proverbs 6. 6–19

The writer of this section of Proverbs has such a keen eye for character. The writer paints a word picture of vice, with deft strokes.

Lord, preserve my eyes, tongue, hands, feet from sin.

1 John 4. 7–end

God is love, and the interpenetration of this love bonds together God with those who love him, those whom he loves, and fellow Christians with one another.

'... the very bond of peace and of all virtues, without which whosoever liveth is counted dead before thee ...' (BCP)

Lord, help me to love those I find it difficult to love.

✳

Thursday evening

Song of Solomon 5.4 – 6.3

Our hearts descend and ascend through the levels of this piece: the physical, the physical in the spiritual, and the spiritual. It is within the realm of the spiritual that the racing, searching heart finds peace.

Matthew 6. 25–end

One thing is needful, and that is to set our minds on God's Kingdom. The rest is needless anxiety.

Lord, draw us back and draw us back again to the still point of adoration.

✠

Friday morning

Proverbs 8. 1–11

Wisdom has its own inbuilt authority and claim, and is accessible to all, through right choice.

'It is to you I call,
to all mankind I appeal' (v. 4).

1 John 5. 1–12

Three witnesses to the verity of Christ are his possession of the Spirit, his water baptism and his 'blood baptism'. This enigmatic claim is set in a whole series of connections between the Son and the Father.

Lord, proof is something I hardly need. Help me to stand by faith.

*

Friday evening

Song of Solomon 7.10 – 8.4

This strange mixture of longing and fulfilment could be editorial, could be experience. We possess love, we lose it, and now we find it again.

' "Let us go up early to the vineyards" (v. 13). Rising from the letter to the Spirit, let us go out to Holy Scripture, where leaves of history nod, the flower of allegory smells sweet, and the fruit of metaphor nourishes' (Alan of Lille).

Matthew 7. 1–14

A gathering of sayings on mercy and compassion leads us to see a compassionate and listening God.

'Ask, and you will receive' (v. 7).

Lord, give me a child-like trust and openness, to share with you what is in my heart.

✠

Saturday morning

Proverbs 8. 12–31

Wisdom is the source of power and authority, and was with the Lord before the creation of the world. Wisdom's co-operation was a matter of delight.

'... and I was daily his delight,
rejoicing always before him' (v. 30, AV).

1 John 5. 13–end

Some large issues come rapidly to a conclusion here. Prayer needs to follow the grain of God's will, and faults, as opposed to deadly sins, can be redeemed through intercession.

Saturday evening

Song of Solomon 8. 5–7

The fire of love is stronger than death. The birthplace and the apple tree have strong echoes of Eden.

'The science of loving ... that is the only kind of science I want' (St Thérèse of Lisieux).

Lord, 'kindle a flame of sacred love, on the mean altar of my heart'. (From Charles Wesley.)

Matthew 7. 15–end

Appearance and reality are set side by side: the rock-like reality of faith in God, and the mere surface acknowledgement of God. The storm reveals the truth.

✠

WEEKDAYS IN WEEK 'C' (PENTECOST)

Monday morning

Proverbs 8.32 – 9.6

Wisdom makes the difference between life and death. In a brief story, Wisdom sets up a home to welcome visitors.

'Great is our Lord and mighty in power: there is no limit to his wisdom' (Ps. 147.5).

1 Timothy 1. 1–11

Far from the murky depths of myths and genealogies is the simplicity and clarity of 'the love which springs from a pure heart'.

*

Monday evening

Baruch 1.15 – 2.10

From exile in Babylon, Baruch justifies the ways of God to man. Their predicament is the result of disobedience.

'In all that he has done to us he is just' (v. 9).

Lord, help us to do your will.

Matthew 8. 1–13

Jesus heals a leper and a centurion's servant, His healings are a response to faith from an outcast and a foreigner.

Lord, I am not worthy that you should come under my roof. You need only say the word and I shall be healed.

Tuesday morning

Proverbs 10. 1–13

The negatives and positives of life are here set out in nuggets of wisdom.

'A prudent son gathers crops in summer;
a son who sleeps at harvest is a source of disappointment' (v. 5).

1 Timothy 1. 12–end

Timothy draws out from his teacher and spiritual friend the confessions of his failures, out of which God wrought the faith we know in St Paul.

'Christ Jesus came into the world to save sinners' (v. 15).

Thank you, dear Lord, for making sinners your first love.

*

Tuesday evening

Baruch 2. 11–27

It must have seemed hard for the exiles to accept that they had to obey the King of Babylon, but that is the word that Baruch receives and has to communicate.

Lord, sometimes we do not understand your will, but from the cloud of unknowing we shoot darts of love.

Matthew 8. 14–17

Diseases, in people who have shown no proof of faith, are cured by Jesus. He embodies the prophecies of Isaiah.

'He took her by the hand; the fever left her' (v. 15).

Lord, heal me, make me whole.

Wednesday morning

Proverbs 11. 1–12

The upright and the wicked are set on opposite balances. The wicked descend and the upright rise. All the problems of ordinary life are dealt with, including the scales themselves.

1 Timothy 2

Prayers are asked for everyone, particularly those with responsibilities in society. We should lift up our hearts in prayer with pure intention, without anger or argument.

'All manner of thing shall be well
by the purification of the motive
in the ground of our beseeching'
(Julian of Norwich).

*

Wednesday evening

Baruch 3. 1–8

Raw beseeching, straightforward crying out to God for help, comes from the heart of Baruch. When prayer has become so rarified, it is helpful to see its roots in basic crying out.

Lord, I cry to you for help.

Matthew 8. 18–27

The world is not for settling in, it is a desert to cross, pulling up our tent at the will of God; and yet that very detachment gives Jesus the power to still storms.

'What sort of man is this?
Even the wind and the sea obey him' (v. 27).

'The Lord sits enthroned above the flood' (Ps. 29.10).

✠

Thursday morning

Proverbs 12. 10–end

Animals, land, and caution in speaking are some of the issues covered by these proverbs. They come within a more general range of good advice.

'The Lord detests a liar,
but delights in honesty' (v. 22).

1 Timothy 3. 1–13

Bishops and deacons need a standard of behaviour which will assist their office and function. The standard is exacting, but bishops are allowed to be married. For bishops we need to understand a more general role, like that of priests today.

'To aspire to leadership is an honourable ambition' (v. 1).

*

Thursday evening

Baruch 4. 5–12

Forgetting the eternal God, and straying into the realms of darkness and dead ends, was Judah's sin. The punishment was exile.

'With joy I brought them up,
but with tears and mourning I watched them go' (v. 11).

Matthew 8. 28–end

The misplaced and corrosive energy of two men is transferred into a herd of pigs who rush to disaster. Those possessed by demons have this uncanny knack of recognizing the presence of God.

Friday morning

Proverbs 14. 9–27

As harvest comes these couplets strike home:

'Whoever despises the hungry does wrong,
but happy are they who are generous to the poor' (v. 21).

'The pains of toil bring grain;
mere talk yields nothing but need' (v. 23).

1 Timothy 3. 14–end

Let us proclaim the mystery of faith. Let us reveal and communicate the secrets by which we live, and on which our faith rests. Jesus is:

'... manifested ... seen ... proclaimed ... believed ... raised' (v. 16).

Lord, help the Church to enter into the life that these mysteries reveal.

*

Friday evening

Baruch 4. 21–30

The God who wields justice also sends joy when he delivers us.

'Take heart, my children!' (v. 27)

Matthew 9. 1–8

The ability to forgive sins and the power to heal were inextricably linked, both for Jesus and his contemporaries. The problem was, who had the authority to administer this healing forgiveness?

Saturday morning

Proverbs 15. 1–17

Right conduct brings joy, and a glad heart. There is a joyous aspect to life for which we give thanks.

'To have a merry heart is a perpetual feast' (v. 15).

1 Timothy 4

There is a great seriousness here expected in the conduct of those who lead: a need to keep close to the scriptures, and to make them an absorbing interest.

Lord, keep me close to where strength really lies, in your word, your silences, your sacraments.

*

Saturday evening

Baruch 4.36 – 5 end

A great hymn of hope and victory is addressed, like Isaiah, to Jerusalem. There is a universal ring to it.

Matthew 9. 9–13

Jesus eats with tax-collectors and sinners. He shocks the religious people by his habits, but he reminds his critics that he expressly came to forgive sins.

WEEKDAYS IN WEEK 'D' (PENTECOST)

Monday morning

Proverbs 15. 18–end

In among the abstract moralism of many of these proverbs, it is helpful to locate one area for thought, a part of the body for example: 'a bright look', 'whoever listens', 'the righteous think before they answer' – eyes, ears and tongue.

1 Timothy 5. 1–16

The position of widows is taken very seriously, and the church community has a special responsibility for them.

∗

Monday evening

Wisdom 1. 1–11

The notion of justice is stronger here than in other wisdom literature, but again, justice is seen as feminine. All human behaviour is spread out before God.

'Even a secret whisper will not go unheeded' (v. 11).

Lord, guard my tongue against futile grumbling.

Matthew 9. 14–17

What lies behind these stories is the something new that appears which makes all the difference: the bridegroom, the new wine, the unshrunk cloth. Jesus is the new thing.

Tuesday morning

Proverbs 18. 10–end

The tongue is often the subject of caution in wisdom literature. In an oral, rather than a literary, culture, the tongue and speaking have increased importance.

Christ's silence before Pilate …

1 Timothy 5. 17–end

The function and character of elders are outlined. Mainly cautionary, the passage suggests that trouble has occurred with the over-hasty laying on of hands.

✳

Tuesday evening

Wisdom 2. 1, 12–22

Sorting out the power of justice, the godless set up a conspiracy to test it. Their wickedness consists in not understanding the depth of God's justice.

Matthew 9. 18–26

One account of a healing is placed in the middle of another to give a sense of time passing. Jesus, in both cases, makes himself available out of a noisy crowd.

'Peace I leave with you, my peace I give unto you' (John 14.27, AV).

Lord, I am not worthy to touch the hem of your garment.

Wednesday morning

Proverbs 20. 1–15

We move from drink, to weights, to the behaviour of children, to attentiveness. Attentiveness is key because wise actions demand thought and care.

'An attentive ear, an observant eye,
the Lord made them both' (v. 12).

1 Timothy 6. 1–10

The writer of this letter encourages us to follow the teaching of Jesus Christ, especially in the area of money. We have to strip ourselves of the love of money before death does it for us.

'We brought nothing into this world, and it is certain we can carry nothing out' (v. 7, AV).

Lord, help me to live lightly to possessions and to be generous.

*

Wednesday evening

Wisdom 3. 1–9

This is a beautiful elegy for the souls of the just, reminding us that their destiny is peace and immortality, and that the Lord will be their King for ever.

Lord, prepare me to attend on you with love.

Matthew 9. 27–34

It is new, and it is full of wonder. The blind receive their sight, and the dumb speak. What was hoped for and prophesied is happening.

Thanks be to God.

✠

Thursday morning

Proverbs 21. 1–13

Much of this proverbial wisdom seems to share the same moral climate out of which arose the teachings of Jesus.

'Whoever stops his ears at the cry of the
helpless
will himself cry for help and not be answered'
(v. 13).

1 Timothy 6. 11–end

Some have noted that this letter does not have the same centrality of the cross as other Pauline letters. God is elevated to great heights.

Blessed and only Sovereign, King of kings and Lord of lords, you alone possess immortality and dwell in unapproachable light.

*

Thursday evening

Wisdom 4. 7–17

Why do people not see the value of doing good? Why do they not consider the fact that the good receive God's grace?

Matthew 9.35–end

It was Ezekiel who lamented for the sheep without a shepherd, and now Jesus laments the lack of labourers for the harvest.

O Lord of the Harvest, send out workers, empowered by you, to work in your harvest.

Friday morning

Proverbs 22. 1–16

The lack of apparent order in these proverbs makes me wonder how they came to be gathered in the way they are. It seems best to take them one at a time.

'A good name is more to be desired than great riches' (v. 1).

2 Timothy 1. 1–7

The handing on of religious influence from grandmother to mother, to son, is a gift which in the first place comes from God.

I give thanks for those who have inspired me and passed on to me such gifts as I have.

✠

Friday evening

Wisdom 5. 1–16

Transience and eternity are contrasted. Vivid images of transience – the bird through the air, the ship through the sea, a shadow – are described. The just, however, live for eternity.

Compare the transient flight of the sparrow from darkness to darkness, in Bede's *Ecclesiastical History* (2.13).

Matthew 10. 1–15

The twelve Apostles are called and sent out on their task, healing and preaching the closeness of the Kingdom. Such simple beginnings – the twelve names still beckon us.

Saturday morning

Proverbs 24. 23–end

An extended moral tale concerns the unweeded garden. Idleness is a strongly condemned fault in these pages. Again you can see some of the proverbs tipping over into the world of the Sermon on the Mount.

'Do not say,
"I shall do to him as he has done to me" '
(v. 29).

2 Timothy 1. 8–end

All the elements of the Pauline letter are here except for the intricate and passionate teaching on the cross. Prison might be wearying him.

Help me, Lord, to keep the treasure of sound teaching, with the help of the Holy Spirit, within me.

*

Saturday evening

Wisdom 6. 1–11

The leaders and rulers will bear the greatest scrutiny by the Lord. Having been given much, much will be expected, by a Lord who has no favourites, and is not swayed by wealth or power.

Matthew 10. 16–25

The demands of an apostolic life at the end of the age involve witnessing before governors and kings, and will demand great endurance.

✠

WEEKDAYS IN WEEK 'E' (PENTECOST)

Monday morning

Proverbs 25. 1–14

An enigmatic opening proverb links up with other scriptural references to the hidden God, for example in Exodus when God hides his face from Moses.

'The glory of God is to keep things hidden' (v. 2).

2 Timothy 2. 1–13

The author leaps from quite mundane pictures of soldiers, athletes and farmers to the hyperbole of 'the glorious and eternal salvation which is in Christ Jesus'.

Pray for the clergy, that while they teach others, they may learn themselves.

Monday evening

Wisdom 7.22 – 8.1

The fluidity of wisdom, its water-like purity and power, conveys a Greek beauty and a Jewish holiness. It is thought that Wisdom was written by an Alexandrian Jew.

Matthew 10. 26–33

Here are a group of sayings to comfort and inspire the apostles. They will be exposed to witnessing but God will care for them, as he does for every detail of creation.

O mercy, a wellspring that can never be exhausted, neglecting neither the young ravens, nor the tiny sparrows.

✠

Tuesday morning

Proverbs 25. 15–end

There are several passages here which commend moderation, but there is also the section which was loved by Jesus: 'If your enemy is hungry, feed him.'

Lord, give me moderation in my own desires, and generosity when it comes to the needs of others.

2 Timothy 2. 14–end

Order in doctrine and order in our personal lives are the concerns here, and they reflect the growing Christian communities striving to be worthy of God's approval.

O Lord, help me rightly to separate out the true gospel.

*

Tuesday evening

Wisdom 8. 5–18

Wisdom is a great treasure, far more valuable than wordly riches. It is the active cause of all things. Wisdom becomes a personal figure to help, and almost to be married to, the one seeking strength to lead and teach.

Matthew 10.34 – 11.1

The sense of total dedication to the cause of the Kingdom of God is very strong, but the rewards are great too, for the committed and those who help the committed.

'Whoever gains his life will lose it; whoever loses his life for my sake will gain it' (v. 39).

✠

Wednesday morning

Proverbs 26. 12–end

Laziness again comes in for severe criticism. Relationships between people are improved by discretion in speech.

2 Timothy 3

Living a Christian life, rather than being a mystical journey, is a holding on to the truths of tradition and scripture, and being good and blameless.

✳

Wednesday evening

Wisdom 9. 5–end

The writer contemplates the intricacy of the world and wonders how it can be understood, unless the Lord had given wisdom and sent the holy spirit of heaven from on high.

Matthew 11. 2–15

Jesus gives his estimate of John the Baptist, and places him in relation to the Kingdom of Heaven.

✠

Thursday morning

Proverbs 27. 1–17

This proverbial wisdom is a whole world. We step in and out of it, and for the most part act intuitively, but occasionally a thought pulls us up short:

'The kisses of an enemy are perfidious' (v. 6).

Lord, we thank you for allowing yourself to be handed over by Judas.

2 Timothy 4. 1–18

The scene is clear. There is a body of teaching which has to be preserved against falsehood, so that those who live by it may stand tall on the day of judgement. Paul is near the finishing line.

'I have run the great race ... finished the course ... kept the faith' (v. 7).

O Lord, bring me to your heavenly kingdom.

*

Thursday evening

Wisdom 12. 12–21

The God of Wisdom rules over all. There is a human heart beating within this power which provide us with lessons for our behaviour.

'By acts like these you taught your people that he who is just must also be kind hearted' (Wisdom 12.19).

Matthew 11. 16–24

Human nature is no guide. God's wisdom is proved right by its results. Matthew never wavers in painting the dark side of faithlessness.

Thanks be to you, O Lord, for willing to be insulted and being falsely called a glutton and drinker.

✠

Friday morning

Proverbs 30. 1–9

Agur's very human lament over his own inadequacy is followed by an acknowledgement of God as protector and acceptance of the simple necessities of life.

James 1. 1–11

To ask God in complete trust for wisdom is a process which humility and poverty make much easier.

'Blessed are the poor in spirit, for theirs is the kingdom of heaven' (Matt. 5.3, AV).

*

Friday evening

Wisdom 13. 1–9

God is the prime author of all beauty, but we fail to see the Creator behind creation, and get distracted by lesser things.

Matthew 11. 25–end

The block is often our own cleverness, but God comes to the simple, and we are welcome to come to God and offload our burdens.

Saturday morning

Proverbs 31. 10–end

Praise in honour of a good woman is set in the context of a family life, and the duties of a household.

James 1. 12–18

Desire, sin, death – the slope downwards is clearly defined. The slope upwards leads to the Father who created the lights, and in whom is no variation.

*

Saturday evening

Wisdom 18. 14–16; 19. 6–9

The glorious sentence anticipating the birth of Christ is this:
'All things were lying in peace and silence, and night in her swift course was half spent, when your all-powerful word leapt from your royal throne in heaven into the midst of that doomed land like a relentless warrior' (vv. 14–15).

Matthew 12. 1–8

Jesus, plucking corn on the Sabbath, was a scandal to the Pharisees, but he rebuts them by appealing to the precedent of David.

'The Son of Man is lord of the sabbath' (v. 8).

WEEKDAYS FOLLOWING WEEK 'F' AT THE END OF PENTECOST

Monday morning

Job 1. 1–12

With all the qualities of a compelling story, the writer sets out a contest between Job and the Adversary: a contest which God allows, and sets the limits of, in order that Job's faith can be tested.

James 1. 19–end

Caution over speech and temper are an indication of faith. Although James is practical – 'look after orphans and widows' – he is also spiritual – 'keep yourself untarnished from the world'.

*

Monday evening

Daniel 1. 1–20

Daniel proves himself an exceptional person in the eyes of Nebuchadnezzar, King of Babylon, who brought Daniel and many others into exile from Israel.

Fasting: if not in sackcloth, yet not in purple and fine linen. If not wholly from all, yet from luxuries. (Lancelot Andrewes, Private Prayers.)

Matthew 12. 9–14

Jesus' healing work is here done under scrutiny and suspicion. It is set in the context of a debate over Sabbath law, but Jesus' authority is confirmed by his healing the man with the withered arm.

✠

Tuesday morning

Job 1. 13–end

Disaster strikes the livelihood and the very lives of Job's family, but he neither sins nor complains to God.

'We brought nothing into this world, and it is certain we can carry nothing out' (1 Tim. 6.7, AV).

Blessed be your name, both now and always.

James 2. 1–13

There must be no discrimination against the poor in favour of the rich. The sovereign law of scripture is 'Love your neighbour as yourself'.

Help me Lord to keep a bias to the poor.

*

Tuesday evening

Daniel 2. 25–45

Daniel helps Nebuchadnezzar understand his dreams, which include the vision of a Kingdom that will stand for ever.

'There is in heaven a God who reveals secrets' (v. 28).

God of Gods, and Lord of Lords, rule my life.

Matthew 12. 15–21

Jesus is attempting to find quiet to escape from the crowds, and the attention which his healing power has brought him. The expectations of God in the writings of Isaiah are becoming a reality.

Wednesday morning

Job 2

In the contest between God and the Adversary in which Job is something of a test case, the trials are made more severe. He is afflicted with 'running sores', 'sore boils' (AV).

James 2. 14–end

A faith without action is a useless thing.

As with Abraham, may faith be at work in our actions, and by these actions may our faith be perfected.

*

Wednesday evening

Daniel 3. 14–20, 24–28

The burning fiery furnace has tested the faith of Shadrach, Meshach and Abed-nego who refused to bow down to any god other than the Lord God.

'It is our God whom we serve' (v. 17).

As you delivered the three children from the furnace, so deliver us, O Lord.

Matthew 12. 22–32

Controversy rages over Jesus' power to cast out demons. He is accused of demon possession himself. The Holy Spirit is the test, the central point of truth, equating the Spirit with 'the finger of God'.

'Over again I feel thy finger and find thee.'
(G. M. Hopkins, 'The Wreck of the Deutschland')

✠

Thursday morning

Job 3. 1–3, 11–17, 20–23

The work takes on a new style, and Job finds a voice. Rather than being a righteous cipher for God's confidence, Job turns and begins his complaint.

Lord, there are times I feel like this.

'There is no peace of mind, no quiet for me; trouble comes, and I have no rest' (v. 26).

James 3. 1–12

So much emphasis in biblical morality is on the danger of words and speech. The tongue is seen as the most dangerous part of the body.

O Lord, I go wrong again and again. Let your mercy 'rejoice against' your judgement.

*

Thursday evening

Daniel 4. 8–18

Nebuchadnezzar shares his dream with Daniel (now Belteshazzar) and, like us, Daniel is bemused by it: a tree, beautifully evoked, the destruction of the tree – and someone, once great, becomes human and degraded.

Matthew 12. 33–37

The appearance is one thing, the interior reality another. It is the truth within that matters. Thoughtless words are greatly condemned.

✠

Friday morning

Job 4.1; 5. 1–16

Eliphaz the Temanite recounts conventional religious wisdom to Job, which seems to come as rather misplaced advice under the circumstances. In itself it seems true, at times beautiful, but the context gives it a painful *hauteur*.

James 3. 13–end

We judge wisdom by its fruits: peace-making, pure, straightforward, sincere, rich in compassion, kind.

O Lord help us to sow peace, that we may reap peace.

Lord, it's not what everyone sees me doing that matters, it's what I know is happening inside.

*

Friday evening

Daniel 4. 19–33

Daniel explains the dream, and warns Nebuchadnezzar that his power will wither, and he will become like a beast.

See Blake's painting 'Nebuchadnezzar' 1795.

O Lord let charitable deeds replace my sins, generosity to the poor my wrongdoing.

Matthew 12. 38–42

'The sign of Jonah' is the sign of the resurrection as well as the sign of three days' darkness. The repentance of the Ninevites is offered as an example to the Israelites.

Saturday morning

Job 6.1; 7. 1–11

The Gethsemane cry, the 'terrible' sonnets of the poet Hopkins, the Auschwitz lament of Elie Wiesel – and here, in the same agony, Job.

James 4. 1–12

The age-old problem of desire and envy leading to actions that bring about struggle, conflict, and war – but the grace of God overcomes this.

'But the grace he gives is stronger' (v. 6).

*

Saturday evening

Daniel 5. 1–6, 13–17, 23–30

The writing on the wall, Belshazzar's feast, the Medes and the Persians: these are the classic trappings of a story about the desecration of the holy things of the Temple.

Matthew 12. 43–45

Daily awareness and caution are needed over the return of the evil spirit that we thought we had overcome.

Lead us not into temptation.

✠

WEEKDAYS FOLLOWING WEEK 'G' AT THE END OF PENTECOST

Monday morning

Job 8. 1–13

Bildad says that people get what they deserve, and wisdom lies in listening to the past and to former generations.

James 4.13 – 5.6

A severe series of complaints against the misuse of wealth is directed to the reader. It compares with the Gospel parable of the farmer who said, 'Eat, drink, and enjoy yourself' when his barns were full, forgetful of his soul.

O Lord, my prayer should begin and end, 'if it be your will'.

*

Monday evening

Daniel 6. 10–end

Daniel was thrown into the lions' den and yet escaped unharmed. King Darius is converted to support 'the God of Daniel, for he is the living God, the everlasting'.

May I pray as Daniel, who knelt down three times a day, and offered prayer and praises to you.

Matthew 12. 46–end

Jesus redefines the concept of family from blood relations, to include those who do the will of his heavenly Father.

Tuesday morning

Job 9. 1–2, 14–24

Job's acute and ruthlessly honest assessment of God's apparent inequality of treatment leaves us thinking, 'how contemporary the tone of voice'.

James 5. 7–end

Patience, prayer, and praise: the farmer's patience as he waits for his crops to grow; prayer on behalf of the troubled; and praise by those whose hearts are full of joy in the Lord.

Lord, give me the insight, planning and humility to say 'no' at the right times, for your sake.

*

Tuesday evening

Daniel 7. 2–14

The great drama of the final judgement is played out among four beasts, the Ancient of Years, and, as fresh and miraculous as the dawn breaking, 'one like a human being' coming on the clouds of heaven. The echoes between this chapter and the Gospels is very strong.

Matthew 13. 1–9

Calculating the effect of the preaching zeal of the gospel, the early Christians realized that it was not all success; but the few who heard and received the word in the good soil of faith, flourished for God.

✠

Wednesday morning

Job 11. 5b–19

Zophan the Naamathite begins here with a line of thought that is much like Job's at the end, but then speaks as the classic Job's comforter; 'If only you had directed your heart rightly ...'

'Life will be lasting, radiant as noon,
and darkness will be turned to morning'
(v. 17).

Galatians 1. 1–10

'Where does this power come from?' is the question to which Paul, with the greatest confidence, gives the answer: from God, seen in the raising of Jesus from the dead.

'When you are brought low by the onslaught of temptation, that you think there is no comfort or help to be had ... you shall suddenly rise in gladness like the morning star, and ... have a sure trust in God.'

(Walter Hilton, *Ladder*)

*

Wednesday evening

Daniel 7. 15–27

The holy ones of the most high are favoured in the sight of God, and reign supreme over the 'beasts' of the nations and the 'horns' of violence.

Matthew 13. 10–17

The teaching of Jesus divided people into those who, through faith, allowed the word to seed and those who hardened their hearts against it.

'To you has been granted to know the secrets of the kingdom of heaven' (v. 11).

Thursday morning

Job 14. 1–14

This ode on mortality has a stoic, realistic tone, 'that has echoes in the sad poetry of every age' (G. G. Bradley); but the final two verses strike a different note and include one of the references, in the Old Testament, to a state beyond death.

'Man that is born of woman hath but a short time to live'.

(From the Burial Service, *Book of Common Prayer.*)

Galatians 1. 11–end

Paul has this overwhelming sense of Christ within and working through him as the inspiration for his proclamation.

'I went off to Arabia ...' (v. 17)

Lord, teach me the rhythm of your presence: desert, indwelling, proclamation.

✳

Thursday evening

Daniel 9. 3–19

Daniel, reading Jeremiah about the wasteland that was Jerusalem, puts down his reading, and is moved to pray. He does this out of his heart for his people.

'Lord, hear; Lord, forgive; Lord, listen and act.'

Matthew 13. 18–23

The disciples here explain to themselves the parable which Jesus told, perhaps on a walk. He cast his words like seeds, hoping they would fall in the soil of his disciples' hearts.

Lord, help me to hear the word with my inner ear, understand it, and let it grow within me.

Friday morning

Job 15. 1, 17–end

Eliphaz recounts what he has seen and what has been handed down in the tradition of wisdom. Wickedness bears within it the seed of its own destruction, and the response of Eliphaz is righteous indignation.

Galatians 2. 1–10

Paul sees himself as an athlete for Christ, fighting for the freedom of all to be released from the narrow demands of the Jewish law on circumcision.

Lord, let us give thanks for the freedom we enjoy in the fellowship of Christ Jesus.

*

Friday evening

Daniel 10. 2–19

After a period of fasting and withdrawal Daniel, in a state of fear and physical weakness, is overcome by a vision of glory. After that, a human hand and touch lift him up and give him strength.

Speak, Lord, for you have given me strength.

Matthew 13. 24–30

A parable of judgement reminds us that God is the judge, and that our human frustration with the patience of God who seems to leave his judgement for so long will find an answer in the end.

Lord, give me patience with your ways.

Saturday morning

Job 16. 1, 12–end; 17. 11–end

It is easy to allegorize this sort of material, but to read it as real is to remember the physical and emotional suffering of many in our world today.

Galatians 2. 11–end

The Jewish–Gentile issue is very strongly in Paul's mind, and leads him to the deepest thoughts about the difference between law and faith in Christ Jesus.

Saturday evening

Daniel 12. 1–4

Couched in an air of secrecy, the events of the end are delivered by a messenger: anguish, the book of names, the division of people, and the wise guides who 'will be like stars for ever and ever'.

Matthew 13. 31–35

Yeast grows quietly in the bread. The secrets of the kingdom are revealed by Christ Jesus. Both yeast and parable transform.

WEEKDAYS FOLLOWING WEEK 'H' AT THE END OF PENTECOST

Monday morning

Job 18. 1, 5–end

A vivid, doom-laden picture is painted of those who care nothing for God. The picture is reminiscent of the paintings of the Dutch painter Hieronymous Bosch, or the *Inferno* of Dante. The parable is a pointed one, directed by Bildad's finger at Job himself.

Galatians 3. 1–14

The Spirit comes through faith in Christ, not through faithful adherence to the law. The Jewish law, because of its impossible demands, holds out no hope. Everyone would fail its demands and be crushed. The curse, Jesus took on himself on the cross.

*

Monday evening

1 Maccabees 1. 10–15, 20–28

So begins a history of the Jews from the accession of Antiochus Epiphanes (175 BC). The Temple is desecrated, the Holy of Holies is stripped, and blood is shed.

'Great was the mourning throughout Israel' (v. 25).

Matthew 13. 36–43

Matthew often emphasizes the extremes of Jesus' teaching: the joys are more joyful and the punishments more terrible. The good and the bad are severely divided.

Darnel: a deleterious grass, which in some countries grows as a weed among corn.

'The righteous will shine like the sun in the kingdom of their Father' (v. 43).

Tuesday morning

Job 19. 13–end

As so often in Job, there is a variety of standpoints in one chapter: terrible but explicable suffering; the suffering that comes from being touched by God; and trust in the redeeming power of God.

I know that my Redeemer liveth, and that he will stand up at the latter day upon the earth.

Galatians 3. 15–end

There are two worlds which pivot on the death of Christ: the world of law with its rules, and the world of life in the Spirit.

Lord, I have been baptized into union with you, have put you on like a garment, am one person with all others who love you.

Tuesday evening

1 Maccabees 1. 41–53

The edicts of Antiochus drove the Israelites into hiding. Their law, customs, and their lives were at stake.

Lord, I spend a lot of time hiding my faith but you did not hide on the cross.

Matthew 13. 44–52

Vivid miniatures of ordinary agricultural and commercial life – digging, fishing, browsing at market stalls – give us insights into the Kingdom of Heaven.

Lord, turn me from a teacher of the law into a learner in the Kingdom, move me from rules to faith, from knowing the law to loving you.

Wednesday morning

Job 20. 1, 4–9, 22–end

Zohar reiterates his belief that evil conduct has evil consequences: 'God vents his anger upon him and rains on him cruel blows.' As an element of the drama it is often a matter, with the book of Job, of hearing the different voices, and hearing them as a part of oneself.

Galatians 4. 1–11

The passage rests on the distinction between being a slave and being a son. Christ has bought our freedom from slavery, and given us sonship.

The rhythm of prayer: 'God has sent into our hearts the Spirit of his Son, crying "Abba, Father!" '

O Lord, pray through me.

*

Wednesday evening

1 Maccabees 1. 54–end

We witness a holocaust in the years just before Christ, and the setting up of 'the abomination of desolation'. The abomination was probably a graven image of Antiochus himself. The law, the covenant, and circumcision were abolished.

Matthew 13. 53–end

The people discuss the nature and provenance of Jesus' wisdom. Their lack of sympathy and understanding turns to fear and aggression. The seeds of the crucifixion are sown here, and reinforced by the beheading of John the Baptist. Jesus is described in his family setting, and a new light is thrown on him.

✠

Thursday morning

Job 21. 1–16

Job wonders why God allows the wicked to prosper.

A common cry goes up, 'Why should this one, who has harmed nobody, die, and that murderer continue to live?' The apparent injustice, sanctioned by God, leads us into this prayer:

Lord, when human reason can see no more,
let me place my mind in my heart,
and wait in patience and humility
for a clearer vision.

Galatians 4. 12–20

A revealing passage from Paul centres on the providential illness which allowed him to go to the Galatians, and to become deeply involved with them. They are his children.

Lord God, help me to have the form of Christ.

*

Thursday evening

2 Maccabees 6. 18–end

Eleazer, one of the leading teachers of the law, becomes a martyr in the service of Almighty God. To him the food laws were worth dying for.

'To the Lord belongs all holy knowledge' (v. 30).

Matthew 14. 1–12

John the Baptist, uncompromising and prophetic, has been imprisoned by Herod, and now through a fatal whim of Herod's is beheaded. The dancing Salome and the desert prophet could not make a greater contrast.

Friday morning

Job 22. 1–5, 21–end

Eliphaz rubs salt into Job's wounds by blaming him for depravity, which seems undeserved. Then with an about-turn, common in this book, Eliphaz says, 'You will be delivered, because your hands are pure.'

Galatians 4.21 – 5.1

By a logic unfamiliar to us, Paul uses the picture of a child born to a slave and a free-born child to make the distinction between a life lived under the law, and a life lived in the Spirit.

'You ... are children of God's promise' (v. 28).

*

Friday evening

2 Maccabees 7. 20–31

This martyrology of Maccabees contains an episode of an anonymous mother and her seven children. The offspring are all murdered for their obedience to Jewish law.

Matthew 14. 13–21

5,000 people, 5 loaves, 2 fish, 12 full baskets left over, 1 Lord: this story is eucharistic and full of outreach. The Lord feeds those who follow.

'His was the word that spake it. He took the bread and brake it. And what that word doth make it, I do believe and take it' (Elizabeth Tudor).

Saturday morning

Job 23. 1–12

To know God's presence and to be seen by God are two different things. These are the rough sketches of faith in which Job grapples with the nature of God: knowing by faith, but not yet seeing as proof.

Galatians 5. 2–15

The sort of life that you can live in the freedom of the Spirit is rooted in the commandment, 'Love your neighbour as yourself'.

Lord, let me serve others in love.

✳

Saturday evening

1 Maccabees 2. 15–28

The zealous Mattathias, in a fit of righteous indignation, cuts down a Jew who comes to worship at the pagan altar at Modin. Modin was the great centre for the gathering and burial of the Maccabean leaders, situated five miles east of Lydda.

Matthew 14. 22–end

Jesus stills the storm on the lake and the storm of doubt in Peter's breast. True faith is the still centre.

'Take heart! It is I; do not be afraid' (v. 27).

Jesus, Saviour of the world, come to me in your mercy.

✠

WEEKDAYS FOLLOWING THE LAST SUNDAY AFTER PENTECOST

Monday morning

Job 25; 27. 1–12

Bildad has the last word of the friends: God is majestic and man is a worm. Job begins a long discourse, full of deep conviction, calling into question the arguments of his friends. Job claims innocence against all his antagonists.

'I am a worm and no man' (Ps. 22.6).

Galatians 5. 16–end

The two ways are clearly spelt out: the unspiritual and the spiritual. What each generates is clearly seen. At separate times we shall need to meditate now on one, now on the other.

'... fornication, indecency ... debauchery ...
... love, joy, peace ...'

*

Monday evening

1 Maccabees 2. 29–48

The hatred and violence of these skirmishes seem to persist through time. The Jews are fighting for the survival of their faith, tied into its connection with the land. Great threats and slaughter overwhelm them, which all sets the gospel Kingdom in context.

Matthew 15. 1–9

Regard for tradition can be just lip-service to human doctrines. There is that other, extra dimension which Jesus is always pushing us towards: not this, not that, but God's Kingdom, God's righteousness.

Lord, make me bold to defy the sterility of merely human tradition.

Tuesday morning

Job 28. 12–end

The familiar and yet fresh sound of the wisdom literature places God at the centre of creation and of all knowledge, and puts us in our right place as humble worshippers.

'The fear of the Lord is wisdom,
and to turn from evil, that is understanding!' (v. 28)

Galatians 6. 1–10

Forbearance towards each other is the welcome theme: judging yourself against yourself. Some details lead us directly into the Christian life of the early days:

'When anyone is under instruction … especially members of the household of faith …' (vv. 6, 10)

*

Tuesday evening

1 Maccabees 2. 49–50, 65–end

The death of Mattathias in 146 is attended by his sons to whom he addresses his last words. The absolute demands of the law make for great zealousness against all who would threaten its purity.

'Now, my children, be zealous for the law, and give your lives for the covenant made with your forefathers' (v. 50).

Matthew 15. 10–20

There are customs and there is what is at the heart. Customs can neither save you nor destroy you, but what comes from within can. The inner principle is what Jesus is anxious for people to see.

✠

Wednesday morning

Job 29.1; 31. 2–8, 29–end

Job assesses his moral conduct, and finds it adequate. The legal framework for this debate is interesting, and we would benefit from knowing the context for understanding the shifts in argument.

How would I assess the purity of my looking, my speaking, hospitality and openness?

Galatians 6. 11–end

All of Paul's main themes based on his life in Christ in the power of the Spirit come tumbling out. He is so excited and moved by the 'new' creation, which he has experienced himself and longs for others to share.

Lord, things are nothing unless they bear the marks of the cross. Let that be my guide.

*

Wednesday evening

1 Maccabees 3. 1–2, 10–26

Judas Maccabaeus is a great hero of the Israelites. He speaks as David spoke:

'Many can easily be overpowered by a few; Heaven can save just as well by few as by many ... strength is from Heaven alone' (vv. 18, 19).

Matthew 15. 21–28

The Canaanite woman with a troubled daughter wins a great test of faith which even surprises Jesus, and wins healing for her daughter.

Have mercy on me O Lord, son of David.
Lord, help me.
Call to mind, Lord, that even the dogs eat
  the crumbs that fall
  from their master's table.

✠

Thursday morning

Job 32. 1–14

Elihu, the voice of youth, speaks up, and with the assurance of his age claims greater honesty than all those who have preceded him.

Colossians 1. 1–14

'You heard of God's grace ... the Spirit has awakened in you ... new growth ... the gospel is bearing fruit.' The thrill of the early Church at work and at prayer is seen here, like looking down a microscope at new life.

*

Thursday evening

1 Maccabees 4 (1–5), 6–25

Judas Maccabaeus routs Gorgias and his 5,000 men.

'That day saw a great deliverance for Israel' (v. 25).

In danger and in difficulty I know, O Lord, there is one who liberates and one who saves.

Matthew 15. 29–31

Jesus' ministry was one of healing and love. That is amazing when you think of all the other things it might have been, in hands less skilled.

God of Israel, I praise you.

Friday morning

Job 35

Elihu seems to be getting quite angry with Job for misunderstanding God. The one constant seems to be God himself, around whom all these people are trying to make sense of their own limited vision. Truth seems to rest with the most compassionate and honest struggle.

Lord, in the middle of struggle, what do I honestly believe?

Colossians 1. 15–23

Placing Christ in creation from the very beginning stretches our rational mind to the limit, whereas our imaginative faculty takes over and relishes the conjunction of the human to nature and time.

*

Friday evening

1 Maccabees 4. 26–35

The war continues with Lysias and the Gentile army retreating and Judas victorious, giving praise to the Saviour of Israel who by David's hand 'broke the giant's onslaught'.

Matthew 15. 32–end

Seven loaves and a few small fish, 4,000 men, 7 baskets filled with the leftovers: were there two occasions or one occasion remembered differently? In each case the followers are fed, through Jesus' giving thanks for, taking, blessing and breaking bread.

Almighty God, we thank you for feeding us with the body and blood of your dear Son.

Saturday morning

Job 36. 1, 5–21

Whereas we tend to draw out the different strands of suffering and recompense, and discuss them separately, Elihu here manages to put them all together. Verses 16–18 have important things to say about being set apart for justice.

Colossians 1.24 – 2.7

God's purposes are revealed in Christ, and through teaching and preaching these purposes are conveyed to the Church.

'... the full wealth of conviction that understanding brings' (2.2).

Prayer as ... 'something understood' (George Herbert).

*

Saturday evening

1 Maccabees 4. 36–43, 52–59

Judas sets about restoring and purifying the Temple for the grand day when sacrifices are again offered and the people come to worship.

'All the people prostrated themselves in worship and gave praise to Heaven for prospering their cause' (v. 55).

Matthew 16. 1–4

Jesus' impatience with signs must come from the way they detract from 'faith' in God, as God. The resurrection, for which Jonah in the whale is a sign, is unique in its power to reveal the meaning of God.

Lord, help me to believe, while in the darkness of the whale's belly.

The Kingdom Season

WEEKDAYS FOLLOWING THE FIRST SUNDAY OF THE KINGDOM

Monday morning

Job 38. 1–11

Out of the tempest or whirlwind of my own thoughts comes the direct questioning of God. The questions about the creation leave us in a state of humility.

Colossians 2. 8–15

Christ the Victor leads the procession of captives: not ordinary prisoners but the cosmic powers of darkness.

'In Christ dwelleth all the fulness of the Godhead bodily' (v. 9).

*

Monday evening

1 Maccabees 6. 1–13

Antiochus suffers two blows, one in Persia at Elymas, and the other he hears at second hand: the defeat of Lysias in Judaea. These break his spirit and he falls ill.

Matthew 16. 5–12

Confusion is rife among the disciples as they struggle to distinguish literal truth and the language of metaphor that Jesus likes to use. So, leaven is not baker's leaven, but the insidious influence of the Pharisees.

✠

Tuesday morning

Job 38. 12–21

A beautiful hymn to the dawn is set in the context of a challenge in our relationship to God. The irony of the final lines sets us thinking about the nature of the writing itself, and how Jesus eschews that sort of ironic tone even to his enemies.

'… to bring up the horizon in relief as clay
under a seal,
until all things stand out like the folds of a
cloak …' (v. 14)

Colossians 2. 16–end

The sub-culture contains quite a lot of shadowy elements, most of which are peripheral and misleading, whereas 'reality' is Christ's.

Lord, help me to focus on you only.

✳

Tuesday evening

2 Maccabees 12. 38–end, 13. 9–17

Great acts of devotion are performed by Judas Maccabaeus over the slain, in the hope of the resurrection for the faithful, and more victories are won with the help of the Lord.

Just Judge and Revealer of Secrets, blot out all traces of offence from us.

Matthew 16. 13–20

This is a classic text on the nature of Jesus, locating him as Son of Man in his own eyes, Christ in Peter's; and the whole discussion is couched in an air of secrecy. In this Gospel, praise and authority is given to Peter.

Wednesday morning

Job 40. 1–14

We simply do not have the means to save ourselves.

Lord, we have no means of ourselves to help ourselves; save us.

Colossians 3. 1–11

Christ is all in all and in us, and that makes all the difference to life: to the way we see other people, and the way we see our life, its direction and priorities.

*

Wednesday evening

1 Maccabees 7. 4b–7, 25–32

Demetrius is approached to destroy the Israelites. He sends Nicanor to trick the Israelites, but the plan is seen through and Judas Maccabaeus remains victorious.

Matthew 16. 21–end

The future contains suffering and death for Jesus, and renunciation for his followers.

'What will anyone gain by winning the whole world at the cost of his life?' (v. 26)

*

Thursday morning

Job 41. 1–11

The majesty of God continues to be described rhetorically. No, we never shall be able to stand up against God.

Colossians 3. 12–17

The nature of the Christian personality in community is set out here with the utmost beauty, with love as the bond and the completion of the whole.

*

Thursday evening

1 Maccabees 9. 1–18

'Judas was among the fallen': simply and starkly put, after all his bravery and zealousness for the purity of the Israelite faith.

Matthew 17. 1–13

To Peter, James and John is given a vision of Christ in glory, flanked by Moses and Elijah. This window on to heaven was granted them as a foretaste of what is to come at the resurrection.

Lord, let me see your glory: glory as of the only begotten of the Father.

'Stand up; do not be afraid.'

✠

Friday morning

Job 42. 1–6

There is movement here, as there is with all religious experience, from a sense of being outside to being inside, to being let in on the secret. Job discovers it to be a shift from 'knowing about' to 'seeing'.

'Therefore I yield,
repenting in dust and ashes' (v. 6).

Colossians 3.18 – 4.1

On a more mundane and practical level some advice is given for different relationships, but even here it has an element of exaltation.

... not to ask for any reward, Lord, save that of knowing that we do your will.

Friday evening

1 Maccabees 13. 41–end

'In the year 170, Israel was released from the gentile yoke', under the leadership of Simon, the maker of the siege-engine.

'The Jews entered the city amid a chorus of praise and the waving of palm branches, with lutes, cymbals, and zithers, with hymns and songs' (v. 51).

Matthew 17. 14–23

Faith (with prayer and fasting in Luke) is the missing factor in the disciples' ability to heal. Jesus' frustration reaches its peak against an unbelieving generation.

✠

Saturday morning

Job 42. 7–end

Job is vindicated in the face of his friends, who are criticized by God for not speaking as they ought. Job's fortunes are reversed, his worldly wealth is increased, and he lives out the rest of his long life as a contented man.

Colossians 4. 2–18

As at the ending of any letter, friends and fellow workers are remembered, including Luke. It is suggested that the letter should be sent on to Laodicea. We are encouraged to be aware of who it is we are speaking to, and to be cautious.

Saturday evening

1 Maccabees 14. 4–15

Being able to sit safely in the streets is a great sign of peace for the old men. This is a description of peace which would be longed for by any at war.

Lord, we long to have peace in the streets of our cities.

Matthew 17. 24–end

An obscure passage which sets out to prove that Jesus pays both temple and state tax, but does it as a gift from God. This is a rare private dialogue with Peter.

✠

WEEKDAYS FOLLOWING THE SECOND SUNDAY OF THE KINGDOM

Monday morning

Ezekiel 1. 2–14

Ezekiel's visual imagination takes us from the the Exile into a world of violent light, and also into the twilight world of humans with animal features. Leaf through the Lindisfarne Gospels and the Book of Durrow to see their influence.

Lord, that I may see.

Ephesians 1. 1–10

There is a wonderful rhythm, almost dance-like, existing between God the Father, his Son, Jesus Christ, and us. We are destined for the dance only through the riches of God's grace in the forgiveness of sins.

Thank you, Lord, for the riches of your grace.

✳

Monday evening

Amos 1. 1–2, 6–end

There is no good news to begin with except that God is to take action against all that is wrong in Damascus, Gaza, Tyre, Edom and among the Ammonites. God's anger is addressed to those who are badly treating others.

Matthew 18. 1–4

How people have understood children has changed through the centuries, but the sense in which Jesus sets them as examples is in their humility and purity. These are traits which are also praised in the Sermon on the Mount.

Lord, give me a childlike love of you.

✠

Tuesday morning

Ezekiel 1.22 – 2.2

War and light, noise and a brilliant shining; and one rising from within in human form, as if through a rainbow, shines with the glory of God.

Ephesians 1. 11–14

Christ is central and the Holy Spirit is the pledge, or earnest (AV), of a future blessing from God.

'The author's tone is that of prayer and meditation, rather than argument' (J. N. Sandars).

Tuesday evening

Amos 3. 1–8; 4. 1–4, 11–12

The harshness of God's judgement arises from the wickedness and evil of the people who he has cared for. Effect follows cause as inevitably as fear follows the lion's roar.

Help me, Lord, to keep thinking onwards, for justice among my people.

Matthew 18. 5–19

The demands are high – purity of heart and eye – and beware of causing the downfall of the pure and innocent. The spiritual values are so important, the physical become insignificant.

✠

Wednesday morning

Ezekiel 2.8 – 3.4

Is eating the word of God, metaphor or reality? It may be a way of putting it. Eating means taking into ourselves, 'inwardly digesting'.

'I ate it, and it tasted as sweet as honey to me' (3.3).

Ephesians 1. 15–end

The inward eye looks in on all great benefits of faith. The great sculpted Christs, such as the Ruthwell Cross in Dumfries, reigning in the wind off the Atlantic bear witness to the majesty revealed in these scriptures.

'He put all things in subjection beneath his feet' (v. 22).

*

Wednesday evening

Amos 5. 14–24

Here are the most stringent demands for justice, not sacrifice, for involvement with the community and its poor, and for personal righteousness.

'Indeed let justice flow on like a river, and righteousness like a never failing torrent' (v. 24).

Matthew 18. 10–14

Who are 'the little ones', is a question a bit like 'And who is my neighbour?' The answer lies in our own perception and conscience. 'A little one' is whoever is vulnerable, lost, or sad, and confronts us with their need.

Lord, have I the strength to cope, except by crying for your help?

✠

Thursday morning

Ezekiel 3. 16–end

The judgements of God, always severe, are mediated through Ezekiel the watchman. It is an awesome responsibility, echoed in Jesus' commission to Peter: 'What you forbid on earth shall be forbidden in heaven' (Matt. 16.19).

Ephesians 2. 1–10

All that is going on inside us is set in the context of the universe as a whole. There is a wideness to the vision, centred on us in Christ, but reaching to the very boundaries of God's world.

'We are God's workmanship' (Tyndale).

*

Thursday evening

Amos 7. 10–end

A thrilling response comes from Amos to the criticism of Amaziah, the priest at Bethel. He was only a herdsman and a fig-grower, but the Lord spoke to him, and … what courage!

Matthew 18. 15–20

Practical answers to the problem of disputes among fellow Christians suggest a quiet and speedy treatment. The small group is very important.

'For where two or three meet together in my name, I am there among them' (v. 20).

Friday morning

Ezekiel 8

Abominations abound, based on the worship of idols. The whole scene is foul, and one longs for fresh air after a visit, even though only in a vision, to the court where various idolatrous practices were taking place.

Ephesians 2. 11–end

Christ has broken down the wall of human division, so that in him we may be one.

Christ Jesus, you are our sacrifice, our peace, and our corner-stone.

'Christ is our peace.
He has reconciled us to God
in one body by the cross.
We meet in his name and share his peace'
(ASB).

*

Friday evening

Amos 8. 1–12

The basket of summer fruit denotes that the time is ripe – never, in Amos, in a mystical sense, but as a sign of the judgement of God on injustice.

Matthew 18. 21–end

Because God has forgiven us, without stint and overwhelmingly, so we must forgive others.

Merciful Lord, forgive us our sins as we forgive those who sin against us.

Saturday morning

Ezekiel 9. 1–10, 18–end

The man dressed in linen, with pen and ink at his waist ... wheels within wheels ... movement ... burning embers flung over the city ... the presence of God flanked by cherubims: Ezekiel's imagination is wild, but full of action and multi-dimensional.

Ephesians 3. 1–13

This deeply theological piece which describes the relationship between Christ and the Church and the 'heavenly realms' has a very broad canvas. It is responding to a community which is drenched in cosmic speculation.

'... the unfathomable riches of Christ ...' (v. 8)

*

Saturday evening

Amos 9. 1–4, 11–end

Such terrible words of judgement are hard to countenance, except as a response to sustained, human wickedness. From the scope of this wrath of God, a remnant will be saved to enjoy the delights of a restored Israel.

Matthew 19. 1–12

Jesus reviews the development of the laws on adultery, and looks back to the primacy of the creation story as normative: 'the two become one flesh'. Renunciation of marriage is also a possibility, for the sake of the Kingdom of Heaven.

✠

WEEKDAYS FOLLOWING THE THIRD SUNDAY OF THE KINGDOM

Monday morning

Ezekiel 11. 14–end

'I will put a new spirit within you,' and where does that take effect, but in the heart? Out with the stony heart, and replace it with the softened heart responding to God.

Lord, 'take my heart, it is thine own'.

Ephesians 3. 14–end

The Holy Trinity, the Church, and you, or we, are all bound together. I notice how it takes us through the Spirit to Christ and into the fullness of God. Every word tells, every phrase encourages, the whole lifts us into the fullness or *pleroma* of God.

*

Monday evening

Micah 2

The cruelty of the people is set against the expectations by God of faithfulness. The particularity of the crimes is interesting: 'to strip the cloaks from travellers', at a time when the cloak was one of the few means of warmth.

Matthew 19. 13–15

Jesus' attitude to children seems revolutionary, and all part of the surprise of the Kingdom.

✠

Tuesday morning

Ezekiel 12. 1–16

A theme that runs through scripture is the inability of a rebellious people to see and hear. Ezekiel acts out a prophetic play to bring people to their senses.

O Lord, give me eyes that see you in the sacraments, and ears that hear you in the Word.

Ephesians 4. 1–6

This is the great prayer for unity, with some of the qualities that make for unity: gentleness, patience, and a spirit of love.

*

Tuesday evening

Micah 3

The leaders are addressed, those who are in positions of responsibility in the land, who sell verdicts for a bribe (v. 11).

Matthew 19. 16–22

The commandments are followed not by a question about the neighbour (as in Luke), but with an equally challenging command to go and sell all that you have and give to the poor. The first response was to a lawyer, this to a rich young man.

I remember G. F. Watts' picture, 'For
he had great possessions', and the
telling hand with its rings, weighing
up the call.

Wednesday morning

Ezekiel 18. 1–13, 30–end

The guilt and responsibility for a person's sin are their own. We stand as individuals before God, willed on by him to do well.

'Get yourselves a new heart and a new spirit' (v. 31).

Ephesians 4. 7–16

Within the bond of peace and unity are individual gifts and strengths. Each one of us has a gift (*charisma*) which needs to be brought to maturity.

✳

Wednesday evening

Micah 4. 1–7

The Lord loves to settle on a high place, and all the people will journey there and find peace.

'They shall beat their words into plowshares, and their spears into pruninghooks: nation shall not lift up a sword against nation, neither shall they learn war any more' (v. 3, AV).

Matthew 19. 23–end

Reversals and seeming impossibilities abound in this powerful description of the demands of the Kingdom.

Thursday morning

Ezekiel 24. 15–end

The sudden death of Ezekiel's wife, as a symbol of the rapid and imminent destruction of Jerusalem, does not even allow tears or the rituals of mourning.

Ephesians 4. 17–24

Learning Christ is learning truth, and this involves a new way, renewed in mind and spirit.

*

Thursday evening

Micah 5. 1–9

One of the great texts on which the birth story in Matthew's Gospel is built, is here: 'Bethlehem in the land of Judah, you are by no means least among the rulers of Judah – for out of you shall come a ruler to be the shepherd of my people Israel' (Matt. 2.6).

Matthew 20. 1–16

The surprising values of the Kingdom are brought out again with the story of the giving out of wages.

'The last will be first, and the first last' (v. 16).

Friday morning

Ezekiel 28. 1–10

The prophet speaks against those who through the amassing of great wealth imagine they are God.

'What, are you wiser than Daniel?' (v. 3)

Ephesians 4. 25–end

Anger, stealing, offensive talk all grieve the spirit of God. The picture is built up of a genuine Christian character.

*

Friday evening

Micah 6. 1–8

The memory is an important divine part of ourselves, as we call to mind the gifts of God. So also is our freedom to choose the future, and what is that? 'Only to act justly, to love loyalty, to walk humbly with your God' (v. 8).

Matthew 20. 17–19

A turning point: Jesus' face is set towards Jerusalem, but on the way he shares the vision of his destiny with his disciples.

✠

Saturday morning

Ezekiel 33. 7–20

Righteousness and wickedness see-saw in the relationship between God and man, but God is on the side of righteousness, and draws people on into a future of greater righteousness.

Help me to do right that I may live.

Ephesians 5. 1–14

In a discussion of the behaviour expected of Christians, the author concludes with the image of light – 'now as Christians you are light' (v. 8) – and with the fragment of an ancient hymn:

'Awake, sleeper
rise from the dead
and Christ shall shine upon you'
(Eph. 4.14).

'Gently move him into the sun'
(Wilfred Owen).

*

Saturday evening *Micah 7. 8–end*

There is a general sense of hope and goodwill in this passage. God and the people are coming to terms with one another, and God will forgive sins and show compassion.

Matthew 20. 20–28

The Kingdom is of perennial interest to the disciples, but they do not fully understand its nature. Jesus has to assure them that human ambition is out of place there. Leadership and authority demand service.

✠

WEEKDAYS FOLLOWING THE FOURTH SUNDAY OF THE KINGDOM

Monday morning *Ezekiel 36. 16–32*

Verses 23–28 are well known from the ASB confirmation service reading. 'Ezekiel is feeling his way in his understanding of the process by which Israel is to be regenerated, foreshadowing the fuller doctrine of the New Testament, especially that of St Paul' (G. A. Cooke).

Ephesians 5. 15–end

The joy and lightness breathe the breath of heaven: 'let the Holy Spirit fill you'. There is a purged, Shaker feel to the idea of music, and a saintly giving of thanks for all things.

*

Monday evening

Ecclesiastes 1

The sceptical world-weariness of Ecclesiastes has often been noted. It seems to work on the level of being a springboard to acceptance of the primacy of God after acknowledging the inadequacy of human wisdom. In some ways it is one long sigh.

Matthew 20. 29–end

Physical sight and spiritual intuition always seem to go together in the Gospel healing miracles. The one sparks off the other. A physical cure and a spiritual awareness of Jesus as Lord are part of the wholeness.

Tuesday morning

Ezekiel 37. 1–14

This is a reading for renewal. What better image than a body building itself back up on to a skeleton, and the breath of life breathed into it?

'Can these bones live?'

Ephesians 5. 21–end

The relationship between husband and wife reflects the Christian's link with the Church. It is as intimate as it possibly can be, and it is mutually loving.

'... an honourable estate instituted of God himself, signifying unto us the mystical union that is betwixt Christ and his Church' (BCP).

Lord of the mystical union, help us to reverence the Church, so the Church responds to that reverence.

*

Tuesday evening

Ecclesiastes 2. 12–23

The pursuit of human wisdom is of no consequence since death makes it irrelevant. Only in God do activities make sense.

'For without God who can eat with enjoyment?' (v. 25)

Matthew 21. 1–11

'Tell the daughter of Zion, "Here is your king ..."' Zechariah's prophecy is fulfilled, realized, made real before the eyes of the Jerusalem crowd. '"The daughter"? God's people, Israel, the Bride of God' (J. C. Fenton).

Wednesday morning

Ezekiel 37. 15–end

Another dramatic act, or miniature play, presses home the point to the people: the leaf of Joseph and the leaf of Judah are to be one, one folding book.

Lord, help us find imaginative ways to express your will to your people.

Ephesians 6. 1–9

Despite the culturally conditioned view of slaves, the sense of unity and service and the mutual bond of love which had been worked out theologically is here presented for our everyday relationships.

*

Wednesday evening

Ecclesiastes 3. 1–11

This well-known passage on time seems to deny any sense of the absolute, except the impossibility of knowing everything created by God.

'He hath made every thing beautiful in his time: also he hath set the world in their heart' (v. 11).

Matthew 21. 12–17

Jesus is in Jerusalem by day, and Bethany by night. The Temple is the centre of his work where he performs the prophetic act of overturning the tables, and teaches, obliquely, about his Messiahship.

Hosanna, Lord Jesus; save me, holy descendant of King David.

✠

Thursday morning

Ezekiel 40. 1–4

'We can imagine Ezekiel pouring over architectural plans and regulations for worship, when he fell into an ecstasy, and seemed to be transported from Babylon to Israel, and set down upon a mountain. There, in the spirit, he sees a building like a walled city; it turns out to be the Temple' (G. A. Cooke).

Ephesians 6. 10–end

God's armour to strengthen us against all wiles or stratagems of the devil includes truth, the gospel of peace, faith and salvation.

Thursday evening

Ecclesiastes 6

Unless God gives the power of enjoyment, however luxurious or prolific the thing is, it is futile.

Matthew 21. 18–22

Signs of faith include a cursed fig-tree, and a moved mountain. Out of the smallest scrap of faith God can do wonders.

Friday morning

Ezekiel 43. 1–9

Ezekiel's overpowering awareness of the glory of the Lord, in the inner court of the Temple, is also an awareness of the dangers of idolatry.

Jude 1–16

The threat to orthodoxy comes in bizarre ways: the defiling of bodies, flouting authority, and insulting celestial beings. Various Old Testament characters appear: Michael, Balaam, Korah, Enoch, Cain and Adam.

'Jesus Christ ... Master and Lord' – the test of right doctrine and a sign of the Spirit.

*

Friday evening

Ecclesiastes 11. 1–8

This is a series of proverbs advising caution, common sense, and hard work.

'However many years a person may live, he should rejoice in all of them' (v. 9).

Matthew 21. 23–27

The ability to understand Jesus' authority rests on a prior ability to understand the nature of John's authority. Jesus' elusive return of question for question is to avoid being trapped in surface conflict, and implies what he claims to be true, that both John's and his authority are from God.

✠

Saturday morning

Ezekiel 47. 1–12

Water is a fecund image of God's life and creativity, and here, most importantly, it is flowing from the sanctuary.

'The water for them flows from the sanctuary; their fruit is for food and their leaves for healing' (v. 12).

Jude 17–end

'I bind unto myself today,
the strong name of the Trinity' (St Patrick).

'Continue to pray in the power of the Holy Spirit. Keep yourselves in the love of God, and look forward to the day when our Lord Jesus Christ in his mercy will give eternal life' (vv. 20b–21).

*

Saturday evening

Ecclesiastes 11.9 – 12.8

The women grinding the meal, where the blossom whitens on the almond tree; the moon and the stars growing dim: these images are reminiscent of the Gospel descriptions of the end of time, but without the urgency of Mark.

'Remember now thy Creator …
or ever the silver cord be loosed
or the golden bowl be broken'
(Eccl. 12. 1, 6, AV).

Matthew 21. 28–32

What was it about the tax-collector and prostitute that allowed them into the Kingdom of Heaven? Was it because they did not expect special treatment?